TORONTO
PUBLIC
LIBRARY
Sale of this book
supports literacy programs

Praise for Alan Ryan's *On Politics*

"Magisterial. . . . In more than a thousand pages, Alan Ryan, a longtime Oxford professor who now teaches at Princeton, undertakes to introduce the reader to most of the major political thinkers in Western history. . . . The tensions of modern liberal democratic societies are the intellectual motor of the boo^ lively and intellectually engaging. . . . ^ at works of philosophy i^ l brief against the une.

New Yorker

"Ryan's book is a ...ent piece of work, clear . . . and engaging. . . . [T]he reader is wonderfully caught up in an uninterrupted trajectory of thought. . . . [A]nyone remotely interested in political theory will profit from reading or dipping into Ryan's *On Politics*. . . . The amazing thing about Alan Ryan is that he has assembled so much of this in a single place, so accessible in this two-volume reservoir of historical and political knowledge. . . . It's a remarkable experience."

—Jeremy Waldron, *New York Review of Books*

"Epic. . . . *On Politics* comes crammed with smart observations and wise advice. Readers unfamiliar with figures such as Machiavelli, Montaigne, Montesquieu and Marsilius of Padua, or with scores of lesser-known political writers, will profit from its clear explanations and well-crafted prose." —John Keane, *Financial Times*

"One of the many merits of Alan Ryan's monumental new history of political philosophy is that it restores our enthusiasm for politics. . . . Mr Ryan's historical approach helps us at the very least to look at our problems from new angles, and at best to harness the help of history's sharpest minds in producing policies. . . . [A]n impressive achievement: an enjoyable mental workout and an admirable monument to a lifetime of academic toil." —*The Economist*

"Any intelligent general reader would learn much from this work and from the author's way of thinking about politics. . . . *On Politics* is an outstanding and original work." —Oliver Kamm, *Times* (London)

"Provocative, illuminating and entertaining—an exemplary work of philosophy and history whose author's deep learning is lightly worn." —*Kirkus Reviews*

"Remarkably detailed yet highly readable. . . . [C]ontemporary American politics lurk in the background, as Ryan, in this absorbing and edifying read, regularly reminds us of what modern citizens might gain from a deeper understanding of the roots of today's political ideals and loyalties." —*Publishers Weekly*, starred review

ON HOBBES

ABOUT THE SERIES

In *On Politics*, Alan Ryan distilled nearly a half century's career of teaching political theory into a two-volume history of Western political thought that spans three thousand years of history from ancient Greece to the present. Each volume pairs Ryan's trenchant analysis with a biography of a major philosopher, a timeline of their life, as well as key excerpts from their most essential works.

The series includes: *On Aristotle, On Machiavelli, On Tocqueville, On Marx, On Augustine,* and *On Hobbes.*

ALSO BY ALAN RYAN

On Augustine: The Two Cities

On Marx: Revolutionary and Utopian

On Tocqueville: Democracy and America

On Machiavelli: The Search for Glory

On Aristotle: Saving Politics from Philosophy

On Politics: A History of Political Thought: From Herodotus to the Present

Liberal Anxieties and Liberal Education

John Dewey and the High Tide of American Liberalism

Bertrand Russell: A Political Life

Property

Property and Political Theory

J. S. Mill

The Philosophy of the Social Sciences

The Philosophy of John Stuart Mill

ON HOBBES

Escaping the War of All Against All

ALAN RYAN

LIVERIGHT PUBLISHING CORPORATION

A Division of W. W. Norton & Company

Independent Publishers Since 1923

New York / London

Copyright © 2016, 2012 by Alan Ryan

Portions previously published in *On Politics: A History of
Political Thought: From Herodotus to the Present*

All rights reserved
Printed in the United States of America
First Edition

For information about permission to reproduce selections from this book,
write to Permissions, Liveright Publishing Corporation, a division of W.
W. Norton & Company, Inc., 500 Fifth Avenue, New York, NY 10110

For information about special discounts for bulk purchases, please
contact W. W. Norton Special Sales at specialsales@wwnorton.com or
800-233-4830

Manufacturing by RR Donnelley Westford
Book design by Ellen Cipriano
Production manager: Anna Oler

Library of Congress Cataloging-in-Publication Data

Ryan, Alan, 1940–
On Hobbes : escaping the war of all against all / Alan Ryan. — First
Edition.
    pages cm
Includes bibliographical references.
ISBN 978-0-87140-848-8 (pbk.)
1. Hobbes, Thomas, 1588–1679. Leviathan. 2. Political science—
Early works to 1800. 3. State, The. 4. Social contract. I. Title.
JC153.H659.R83 2015
320.1—dc23

                                        2015029300

Liveright Publishing Corporation
500 Fifth Avenue, New York, N.Y. 10110
www.wwnorton.com

W. W. Norton & Company Ltd.
Castle House, 75/76 Wells Street, London W1T 3QT

1 2 3 4 5 6 7 8 9 0

CONTENTS

PREFACE

I N THE INTRODUCTION TO *On Politics*, I suggested that one measure of the book's success would be the readers who went and read the works of the authors I discussed. Some readers suggested that I might encourage them to do so by taking chapters of *On Politics* and adding to them substantial extracts from the works I hoped they would read. What follows is exactly that, with a short introduction to provide some of the context that the chapter's original placement in *On Politics* would have provided. As before, I am grateful to Bob Weil and William Menaker at Liveright, as well as to the Norton production team, for their help in making an author's life as easy as it can plausibly be made.

CHRONOLOGY

1215	King John signs Magna Carta
1265	Henry III calls first Parliament
1485	Battle of Bosworth Field; Henry VII becomes first Tudor king
1509	Accession of Henry VIII (d. 1547)
1558	Accession of Elizabeth I (d. 1603)
1587	Execution of Mary Queen of Scots
1588	Hobbes is born, April 5 (his mother went into labor prematurely on the rumor of the arrival of the Spanish Armada)
1588	August–September, Spanish invasion fleet arrives off Flanders, is driven off, and is subsequently scattered in an Atlantic storm
1602	Hobbes matriculates at Oxford; receives his BA in 1608
1603	Accession of James I (James VI of Scotland) (d. 1625)

1608	Hobbes joins the household of Lord Cavendish (later first earl of Devonshire)
1610–15	European tour with Cavendish's son; travels to France and Italy
1623	Hobbes acts as amanuensis to Francis Bacon
1625	Accession of Charles I
1629	Hobbes publishes translation of Thucydides's *History of the Peloponnesian War*
1634	Takes the third earl (aged 16) to France and Italy
1635	Associates with Mersenne, Gassendi, and others in Paris
1636	Meets Galileo in Italy
1640	Writes *Elements of Law*; fears to be arraigned before Parliament, flees to Paris in November
1640	"Long Parliament" is called in November (purged in 1648; the "Rump" is dissolved by Cromwell in 1653; recalled in 1659; dissolved in 1660)
1641	Contributes to the *Objections* to Descartes's *Meditations*
1642	Civil War begins in March; Hobbes publishes *De cive*
1646	Appointed mathematics tutor to Prince of Wales in Paris
1647	Falls seriously ill in August
1649	Charles I is executed, January 30 (the Anglican calendar still celebrates the feast of Charles Martyr)

1651	*Leviathan* is published in April; Hobbes is dismissed from the royal court in December
1651–52	Hobbes "engages" and returns to England
1660	The Restoration; accession of Charles II (d. 1685); Hobbes is received at court
1666	Threat of prosecution for heresy and/or atheism
1675	Hobbes retires to Chatsworth
1679	Hobbes dies at Hardwick, December 3
1683	Hobbes's works are burned in the Bodleian Quadrangle in Oxford
1685	Accession of James II (abdicated 1688/9)
1688	Accession of William III and Queen Mary

INTRODUCTION

INTRODUCING *ON POLITICS*, FROM which the account of Hobbes that follows this introduction is drawn, I expressed the hope that readers might turn from my account of the writers whom I discussed in that book, and read the work of those writers for themselves. It was suggested to me that I could help this to happen by taking some chapters on particular authors from *On Politics* and adding selections from the works I hoped readers would turn to. This is what I have again done here. Doing it presents one obvious problem. In the book from which the chapters are taken, they are preceded and followed by discussions of other writers that put them in a context, both chronological and thematic. Those discussions also give the reader some idea of the political and intellectual background that influenced the writers I discuss and some idea of their subsequent influence. This preface supplies some of that back-

ground; I begin with a sketch of the tumultuous political events that lay behind Hobbes's obsession with
order and authority; then I move on to explain why he
upset so many of his contemporaries, and why he
deserves his reputation as the political thinker who
most decisively broke with the classical and medieval
past and launched modern ways of thinking about politics and much else. What Descartes meant to philosophy more broadly, Hobbes means to political philosophy
in particular.

Hobbes was born on Good Friday, 1588. By that
time England had become a Protestant country, or more
exactly a country whose ruler, the first Queen Elizabeth, had ensured that anybody who valued his or her
life or property was well advised to profess the Protestant Christianity preached by the Church of England,
the established church of which the monarch was, and
is, the head. How far the population at large was committed to the newly established religion, and to what
extent it missed the old faith, is impossible to guess.
Until the expulsion of James II a hundred years later, it
seemed to many people, from the last Stuart kings
downwards, and to friends and foes, that the reunifica-
tion of the English and Roman Catholic churches was a
plausible ambition. Indeed, from 1690 to 1910, it was
required of British monarchs at their coronation to
abjure the "damnable doctrine" that monarchs may be

deposed for heresy; this was Catholic doctrine, although the last time a pope declared an English monarch deposed as a heretic was in 1570, and it only made the government's persecution of English Catholics more savage. Even so, in the eighteenth century, the 1715 and 1745 rebellions showed that a Stuart restoration could not be wholly discounted, and with it the restoration of Roman Catholicism as the official religion of the United Kingdom.

In 1588 it was common knowledge that the king of Spain, Philip II, was proposing to launch an invasion of Britain to bring the country back into the Catholic fold. Hobbes's mother went into labor on hearing the ringing of church bells, which she mistook for alarm bells announcing the arrival of the Spanish Armada. In fact, the Armada did not appear until late August, and it was destroyed by poor tactics, superior English seamanship, and violent equinoctial gales. This was the last serious attempt at an invasion of Britain, unless one counts the not entirely peaceful accession to the throne of William III and Queen Mary in 1688–89; William arrived by invitation in November 1688, but he brought an army with him. In 1588 England was far from being a settled, stable, united country. Apart from the dangers posed by Spain, it was increasingly obvious that the queen was not going to produce an heir, and that the Tudor dynasty would become extinct on her death.

Succession crises are a standing hazard of monarchy. Elizabeth reigned for forty-five years, dying only in 1603, but both she and her counselors knew that her father's search for an heir had cost the lives of more than one of his queens, provoked the breach with the Roman Catholic Church, and led to a decade of religious and political upheaval between his death in 1547 and the accession of Elizabeth in 1558. But she remained determinedly unwed in spite of the best efforts of her advisers. Ironically, she was succeeded by the son of Mary Queen of Scots, James Stuart, already James VI of Scotland, and now James I of England. Ironically, because James's mother was imprisoned for eighteen years by Elizabeth, and executed for treason in February 1587; she had arguably had a better claim to the throne than Elizabeth, and was certainly a focus of Catholic hopes, although she was almost certainly innocent of treason. James the Sixth and First was a Protestant, and did nothing to save his mother, either from imprisonment or from execution. He became king of Scotland at one year of age, when his mother had been forced to abdicate; by the age of twenty-one he knew where his interests lay.

Although Hobbes's birth had been brought on by his mother's fears, his childhood and adolescence were disturbed by his father's misbehavior rather than by anything on the wider stage. His father was a clergyman, whom Hobbes's first and greatest biographer, John Aubrey, described as "one of the ignorant Sir Johns of the old Queen's reign." He had a fierce temper, and during a quarrel with a parishioner struck his adversary and was forced to flee his parish. Hobbes's education was then seen to by an uncle who got him a good training in classical languages and sent him to Oxford. From there he went on to be employed by the Cavendish family as secretary and tutor to successive earls of Devonshire; he remained with the family for most of the rest of his life.[1] However, in the run-up to the Civil War of 1642–47, he fled to France, where he remained until 1652, when he returned to England and submitted to the Commonwealth government of Oliver Cromwell. Although the publication of *Leviathan* in 1651 made a breach with his royalist friends, and led to Hobbes's being banished from the exiled royal court in Paris, Charles II was of a forgiving disposition, and Hobbes became a favorite at court after the restoration of 1660. Even so, his religious views made him unpopular, and he eventually retired to the country, spending his last years at Chatsworth in Derbyshire, dying in 1679 at the great age of ninety-one.

The Civil War, the divisions between crown and

---

1 A longer account of Hobbes's career is given below in the chapter taken from *On Politics*.

Parliament that led up to it, and the religious conflicts that had been sparked off throughout Europe by the Reformation and the opposition to it, form the context for Hobbes's attempt to prove, rigorously and incontrovertibly, that political authority must be absolute, and must embrace authority over church as well as state. The sovereign must wield both sword and scepter. Old-fashioned histories depicted the Civil War as a battle between Roundheads and Cavaliers, the "Roundheads" being low-church Puritans and the Cavaliers royalists with a leaning toward high-church religion. The underlying cause was the struggle for power between the crown and Parliament, and the root of their conflict was taxation, although the war was indeed triggered by a rebellion by Charles I's Scots subjects when he attempted to impose the Church of England prayer book on them. The ultimate cause of tension between king and Parliament was that the English crown was chronically short of money; this had been true for over a century. Indeed, the origins of the English parliamentary system lay in the financial needs of Henry III three centuries earlier. Henry VIII's suppression of the monasteries had owed nothing to religious conviction and everything to his need for funds. When the monarch's own resources were inadequate, it was necessary to summon a Parliament and ask it to approve a temporary tax or "subsidy"; Parliament, unsurprisingly, wished for concessions in return; the principle of "no supply without redress of grievances," understood to mean that the crown would agree to remedy grievances presented by Parliament before Parliament granted a "subsidy," was insisted on by Parliament and resisted by the crown. Much though Queen Elizabeth had been loved, she had found herself in the undignified position of having to cajole her Parliaments, and always resented it. The role of a constitutional monarch was anything but congenial to her.

The Stuart kings were even more hard-pressed financially, and still more insistent on the prerogative rights of the monarch. This implied that the king should be able to impose taxation as he saw fit, even if he was *morally* bound to husband his kingdom's resources. Even as he was about to be executed, Charles I reasserted the principle of absolute monarchy, telling his subjects that "their liberty and freedom consists in having government. . . . It is not their having a share in the government; that is nothing appertaining unto them. A subject and a sovereign are clean different things." It was possible to govern without Parliament, since although "subsidies" were off-limits without parliamentary assent, other fees and levies were less dependent on the goodwill of Parliament. When Charles I came to the throne in 1625, the cupboard was bare; Charles had extravagant tastes, became embroiled in unsuccessful continental wars, and married a French Catholic princess, Henrietta Maria. Charles was not a Catholic, covert or otherwise, but favored a more ritualistic Anglicanism than many of his subjects, a proclivity that alienated the Presbyterian Scots. After four years of quarreling with Parliament during the first years of his reign, he ruled from 1629 to 1640 without calling a Parliament. The expedients he employed to raise money in those years embittered much of the population, and the arrogance of his two closest advisers, Archbishop William Laud and Thomas Wentworth, earl of Strafford, did nothing to conciliate them.

The downhill slide into civil war began in 1637 with the attempt to force the use of a new Book of Common Prayer on Scotland; riots turned into rebellion, and a Scots army invaded northern England. In April 1640 the king was forced to call a Parliament; it made unacceptable demands and was promptly dissolved. His position weakening, Charles called another in November 1640. It demanded the dismissal of Laud and Wentworth, and secured the execution of Wentworth and the imprisonment of Laud. More significantly for the long run, it forced Charles to agree that Parliament could not be dissolved without its own agreement, while the Triennial Act laid down that a new Parliament must be called every three years. In fact, the Parliament called in November 1640 was very unwilling to be dissolved at all; this was the famous

Long Parliament, which sat until it was purged by Cromwell's army in 1648, and finally agreed to its own dissolution only in 1660, at the Restoration. Further rebellions in Ireland created more problems for Charles, who found Parliament determined to micromanage the conduct of the Irish war; in August 1642 Charles launched the Civil War by raising an army to crush Parliament. The armies raised by Parliament proved more than a match for his forces. The war ended in 1647 with his defeat, broke out again in 1648, and ended definitively with Charles's execution on January 30, 1649, and the abolition of the monarchy the following month.

Hobbes left for France well before the war broke out. He left as the Long Parliament was called. "I was the first of all that fled," he said, priding himself on his caution as other men might pride themselves on their courage. How right he was to feel frightened, it is hard to say. The cause of his fear was his first political treatise, *The Elements of Law.* He meant it for private circulation in manuscript, but copies circulated more widely, and he heard that Parliament was going to "examine" it and its author; the likely outcome if that had occurred would have been imprisonment and possibly execution. It was unequivocally a treatise in favor of absolutism; Parliament was committed to a "mixed" constitution in which authority was shared. Hobbes remained in France until

1651. Even when the monarchy was restored, in 1660, Hobbes was an object of suspicion: to parliamentarians who disliked the monarchy, to monarchists who disliked his contempt for theories of divine right, and to innumerable others who suspected him of atheism, a charge he always denied. Four years after his death his works were burned in the quadrangle of the Bodleian Library in Oxford, an ironic fate for the works of a man who had hoped they might be preached from the pulpit.

The rest of this introduction will spell out some of the ways in which Hobbes gave offense by so violently breaking with the past and espousing doctrines that were felt to undermine orthodox views of religion and morality. Many of the ideas he broached in *Leviathan* and elsewhere remain contentious to this day, although their exponents are unlikely to be accused of heresy and threatened with death at the stake. The first cause of offense, and one that perhaps embraced all the rest, was Hobbes's contempt for the authority of tradition. Aubrey quoted Hobbes as saying that if he had read as much as other men, he might have known as little as they, which suggests the style as well as the doctrine. "Mr. Hobbes," complained one of his clerical critics, "takes arms against a host of learned men," and so he did. The notion that the antiquity of an idea gave it authority was one he repudiated as energetically as Bentham long afterwards. We should not rely on beliefs that are multiply secondhand. Even if they had been well founded in the first place, the odds against their being transmitted accurately were high. In any case, a man who accepted ideas on trust was like an incompetent owner of an estate who took his steward's accounts at face value and did not go through them for himself. The crucial question was not whether a doctrine was old but whether it was true; and that was a matter on which we must judge for ourselves. The only intellectual authority in Hobbes's view was a man's own intelligence—as long as that intelligence was properly trained, and exercised scrupulously and impartially, as he thought his own was.

A crucial aspect of Hobbes's general disdain for appeals to the authority of the past was his distaste for republican theories of politics. Machiavelli before Hobbes, and innumerable thinkers after him from Sir James Harrington to Jean-Jacques Rousseau and beyond, believed that there was a vast difference between political systems in which rulers might be elected or chosen by lot, but were in any event answerable to the people, and political systems in which they were not. The conspirators who murdered Julius Caesar to reinstate the Roman Republic, did so in the name of liberty. The "Commonwealthmen" who supported Cromwell and instituted the short-lived English republic did so in the name of liberty. Hobbes thought they were talking nonsense. Worse, it was dangerous nonsense. Few things had been more dearly bought than the knowledge of Aristotle and Cicero. Of course, one may have very mixed feelings about Hobbes's brisk dismissal of classical republicanism. His view that "liberty" consists in the silence of the laws and his insistence that freedom is a matter of how far we are left alone by governments are the common sense of modern liberalism, but the idea that liberty "in Constantinople" is identical to liberty in Lucca is more than counterintuitive. In Constantinople everyone is essentially a slave, with no rights; in Lucca everyone—at all events, every adult male of a certain economic standing—is a *liber*, a free man with social and political rights.

Hobbes rode roughshod over all this as over much else. One reason was that although he had translated Thucydides's *Peloponnesian War* in 1629 and declared Thucydides "the most politic historiographer that ever writ," he had concluded that the cause of peace would be served better by a new political science than by the prudential arguments from history favored by republican thinkers such as Machiavelli, Cicero, and the Greek historian Polybius. In *Leviathan* he contrasted "prudence," based on experience, with "science," based on the apt definition of terms and careful deductive inference. Science, conducted properly, was infallible. Just what Hobbes's conception of science was remains contested to this day. We know that he thought of geometry as the paradigm of science; to a modern eye, this is unpersuasive, because we think of geometry as nonempirical and think of the sciences as empirical, and scientific theories as open to refutation by experimental evidence. Before Kepler, planetary orbits were thought to be circular; that assumption was impossible to reconcile with astronomical observation; Kepler resolved the discrepancy when he determined that planetary orbits were in fact elliptical. That is a paradigm of a scientific theory being forced to fit the facts. No such procedure seems to make sense in the case of geometry. Hobbes also thought of science as based on the so-called resolutive-compositive method. We should imagine whatever we are trying to explain as decomposed into its component parts and then reassembled; the analogy is with the watchmaker whose knowledge of how a watch works is demonstrated by his ability to disassemble a watch and then reassemble it. Hobbes, indeed, appeals to just that analogy. We must think of a political society as taken into its component parts—"in imagination only"— and then reassemble it so that it works properly. The component parts are individual men, and a properly functioning state exists when they relate to one another as they should, with their actions dictated by the laws of the society. If one thinks of the watchmaker analogy, the attraction of geometry as a model for a science of politics is understandable; the watch as designed would function perfectly.

If Hobbes's claim that geometry was the only science with which God had seen fit to bless mankind—until Hobbes had created a political science—puzzles the modern reader, his materialism does not. Or rather, Hobbes's materialism, like present-day forms of materialism, is problematic in several respects, but it is not difficult to know what Hobbes means. Everything that exists is material. This is not the same claim as his claim that everything that exists is particular, and that there is nothing universal but names: red objects and the word "red," but no such *thing* as redness. Nonetheless, there is a certain affinity between his nominalism and his materialism. His materialism was all embracing, as one can see by contrasting him with Descartes. Descartes thought that human beings were composed of two distinct substances, mind and matter; their interaction—for instance, when we decide to perform any act that involves deliberate movements of our bodies—was then a puzzle, since it was hard to see how immaterial thought got a material limb to move. On the other hand, it seemed obvious that *thinking*, the activity definitive of the mind at work, was something quite other than the movement of a hand or arm.

Hobbes simply denied that thinking required an immaterial thinking self. Human beings are thinking matter. The idea that matter cannot think is simply superstitious; we are evidently material objects that think. The crux of Hobbes's case is one that resonates with any twentieth-century philosopher. We are like other animals, in essence elaborate machines that are, in the modern jargon, programmed to keep ourselves in existence by interacting with our environment to consume food, avoid danger, procreate, and so on. We are decisively unlike other animals in having acquired a distinctive form of language. Thought, in the sense in which we understand it, is what one might call the subjective side of speech. Like everyone else who has speculated on the subject, Hobbes was unsure how language might have arisen: and it is indeed hard to see how it could have been invented without already existing.

The problem to which Hobbes had no answer, and perhaps for that reason did not raise it in the usual form, is that of consciousness. It cannot be said that anyone has done better in the intervening centuries, and there are more than a few modern philosophers who deny that there can be an answer to the question of how a material object comes to possess consciousness in the sense in which we are, if awake and in possession of our faculties, conscious of how the world looks, feels, smells, and tastes. Like his successors, Hobbes speculates that physical interaction with the world sets off reactions within us, and that we respond to visual, audible, tac-

tile, and olfactory stimuli, as do other animals. That
leaves unsolved the puzzle of the subjective perspective,
of how the world *seems* to us. Hobbes was adamant that
there were no occult entities in the world, such as "visible species" interposed between unknowable objects in
themselves and our senses; we, physical systems, interacted with a material world. He refers to "phantasms"
in the brain, but that transparently will not do as a general answer. It is the experience of the perceiving subject
that needs explaining.

Why might this matter to a political theorist? There
are two reasons, of which the second was in Hobbes's
own day the more important. The first is philosophically
salient today. Hobbes denied the existence of free will; it
is not the will but the man that is free. Freedom is the
absence of external restraints. A man who is not hindered
by anything external in doing what he has a mind to do
and is capable of doing is free. Our actions are both
necessitated and free, just as an unobstructed stream runs
"freely" downhill and is caused to do so by gravity.
Hobbes had strong motives for adopting this definition
of liberty; it allowed him to say that the citizens of so-
called free republics were neither more nor less free than
the citizens of any other form of society, but also and
equally counterintuitively that a man who submits to a
conqueror to save his life does so "freely" and is bound
by whatever agreement he makes at that moment. Hobbes

has resources to argue that agreements made from fear are binding; we agree to pay the baker because we fear to go hungry, and yet we think that we are obliged to pay our bill. Still, it is one thing to pay our baker's bill, another to yield ourselves subject to the baker. In the former case, we remain our own masters; in the latter, not. Even in the former case, we would be much less inclined to think that we ought to pay the baker what he asks if, for instance, he was taking advantage of a food shortage to raise his prices to an extortionate level.

The more immediate problem that Hobbes's materialism caused him was that it cemented his reputation as an atheist. If everything was material, and the world was a *plenum*, which is to say there was no truly empty space, only places filled with very thin matter, it was hard to see what room there was for God. Hobbes did not improve matters by giving a wholly naturalistic explanation of the origins of religion in anxiety, curiosity, and fear of ghosts; because we are anxious, we want to know the causes of events, and where we cannot readily ascertain them, we feign imaginary causes. As to the existence of God, we think there must be a God because we see that the causes of things have further causes, and working our way back through the chain of cause and effect, we conclude that the whole process must itself have a first cause, which we call God. Hobbes was well aware that the first-cause argument was problematic inasmuch as it prompted the

question what caused God. It seems no more satisfactory
to say that everything begins with an uncaused cause
than to say that the chain of cause and effect is endless.
Hobbes's way out was characteristic; he said that whether
the universe was eternal or not was unanswerable by
philosophical argument, and that we should say whatever our sovereign commanded on the subject, although
it insulted God to say it was eternal, because that limited
his creative power. His views did not appeal to the
devout, and Hobbes knew it, but when arguing over free
will and divine foreknowledge with Bishop Bramhall, he
stuck to his guns, maintaining that religion is "law not
philosophy."

Hobbes insisted that he was not an atheist. Nor did
not go down the same track as Spinoza. Spinoza identi-
fied God and nature. He was an avowed pantheist, maintaining that the universe was identical with God; it had
two aspects, creative and created, or *natura naturans* and
natura naturata. Hobbes was reported as saying of Spinoza,
"He hath outthrown me a bar; I durst not be so bold."
Since he was in danger of execution as a heretic, he had
good reason to be cautious. It is not obvious that Hobbes
had any reason to be tempted by Spinoza's pantheism; he
maintained that he held orthodox Christian views, and
his view that the universe was created by an arbitrary and
unintelligible act of God was not in itself unorthodox.
Nor, for that matter, was his "mortalism," his espousal

of the view that at death the soul died with the body; Milton, whose faith nobody has questioned, was a mortalist, as were many of his contemporaries. It was a mark of Hobbes's good nature that he gave a very unusual account of the Last Judgment. It would be not so much a resurrection of the dead as a new birth; once judged, the saved would live forever, apparently on earth, while the damned would simply be annihilated. Milton's Adam would have been reassured.

Few modern readers spend much time with books 3 and 4 of *Leviathan*, and I include only a paragraph here. Most of the issues Hobbes was concerned with, such as the authorship of the so-called Mosaic Books of the Old Testament, have lost their salience; some, such as Hobbes's views on toleration, have not. Put simply, Hobbes insisted that since we could know nothing about God other than he was all-powerful, what mattered was that men should worship him in whatever way did him honor according to the local conventions established by the sovereign. Religion was law, not philosophy; the avoidance of contention was fundamental. This meant, among other things, that persons who thought they had divine authorization to establish a new political order had to be suppressed, not because they were heretics but because they threatened the peace. The concept of heresy was one on which Hobbes had strong views, unsurprising in someone whom the bishops had wished to burn as a heretic. His view was that "heresy" simply meant a doctrine that contradicted what the church preached, and that only priests were under any obligation to believe the church's doctrines. What Hobbes also thought, and what narrowed the range of what we might say in public, was that whatever the sovereign authority commanded us to say, we should say.

This, interestingly, made Hobbes an unlikely friend to a substantial measure of toleration. He was not a liberal. We have no *right* to toleration; our rights are whatever the sovereign authority says they are, and we must accept that what may be said publicly is whatever the sovereign allows. But Hobbes's whole system was based on fear; our willingness to obey the sovereign's commands springs from our fear of the harm that other men might do us in the absence of a strong sovereign. If we think the sovereign's views may imperil our salvation, we are bound to be frightened to obey him, even if we think that God will forgive us for saving our skins by saying what we do not really believe. The sovereign should therefore not inquire into what his subjects really think, especially if he realizes that his subjects can easily lie about their beliefs. In the English *Leviathan* Hobbes drew the conclusion that *if* it could be done without contention, everyone should be free to follow whatever preacher or church he chose.

Finally, then, the feature of Hobbes's political theory that everyone remembers most clearly. Hobbes's belief that the way to understand politics was to imagine the state reduced to its components and then reassembled led him to consider what men might be like in a "state of nature." This was a novelty in the form in which he presented the argument. The "state of nature" was a pure theoretical construction. He knew that mankind had never lived in such a condition, and offered the picture as an account of what human beings *would* be like if they interacted without a political authority to keep them in order. The obvious analogy is with the modern economic theory of perfect competition; there never have been perfect markets or perfectly informed and rational agents, but we can build illuminating economic models by imagining their interaction. Hobbes argued that, absent a sovereign, there would be a war of all against all. Rational agents *must* see one another as enemies, and take steps not to fall prey to them; but this means that the belief that we are enemies to one another is true, since the best means of avoiding falling prey to other men is to disable them before they can strike.

Rational men who do not *wish* to fight one another, but discover that in the absence of an authority to "overawe them all," they *must* do so, also know what the solution is. They need to live under law. The content of that law is, in outline, natural law, which is to say rules found out by reason. But one of Hobbes's most striking achievements was to transform what natural law meant. Hobbes held what legal theorists call an imperativist theory of law; law is "the word of him that by right hath command." In the state of nature all of us or none of us have such a right; God rules by that right, since he is all-powerful. We are equals, and since we each have the same right to all things, we have a right to command that is perfectly useless and indeed incoherent, since we each have the right to command everyone and no ability to exercise that right, and a duty to obey that would get us killed, and can be no duty. So, what are the laws of nature? The answer is that they are not laws but "theorems." Until they are actually the commands of a superior, their status is that of well-founded claims about what rules we *should* obey. But, Hobbes goes on, if we think of them as the commands of God, who by right commands all things, they are properly laws. In other words, "nature" cannot issue commands; "nature" is not normative, but just the way things are. God can issue commands, but they will not be effective until there is an earthly sovereign to enforce them. The bleakness of the argument is the effect of abandoning the teleological conception of the universe common to the classical and medieval worlds, and destroyed by the new physical science. Hobbes was the political thinker who embraced and embodied that transformation.

ON HOBBES

Hobbes: Escaping the War
of All Against All

MODERNITY

WHEN VIRGINIA WOOLF WROTE that "on or about December 1910, human nature changed," she was being playful and provocative. When historians of ideas and political theorists debate whether it is Hobbes or Machiavelli, or neither, who is to be counted as the first "modern" political thinker, they are usually being wholly serious. This is not to say that any particular candidate is universally accepted as the first modern thinker or that the question is universally thought to make a great deal of sense; the grounds for proposing one or another writer as the first modern thinker necessarily implies a debatable view of what constitutes "modernity." It is unfair to both Machiavelli and Hobbes to attempt an evenhanded resolution of such a debate; Machiavelli praised himself for bringing a "new method" to the discussion of politics, and Hobbes declared that political science was no older than *De cive*. The view that animates this part of the book is that to the extent that the question makes sense, modernity begins with Hobbes. The grounds for skepticism about the question are many, not least among them the hankering after the political practices of the ancient world that persists to this day.

The thought that modernity begins with Hobbes is this. Machiavelli was essentially a backward-looking figure. His ideal of a successful political regime was the Roman Republic. His ideas about what made Rome the success it was were much the same as Polybius's and would not have surprised Pericles. Rome was stable, law-abiding, the military superior of any power on earth; its citizens were loyal, public-spirited, courageous, and self-disciplined. Machiavelli says nothing about the intellectual, literary, artistic, or architectural glories of Rome, other than to complain that his contemporaries copied statues but did not copy great men. Although his *Discourses* is a commentary on Livy's *History of Rome*, Machiavelli does not have the modern sense of history as an irreversible process in which our forebears become increasingly remote from us and decreasingly intelligible to us. History is a storehouse of *exempla*, and the underlying thought is that what has worked in one time and place will work everywhere.

Although Hobbes does not appeal to the idea of progress as later writers did, and does not write the panegyrics to the value of science in easing man's estate that his former employer Francis Bacon did, he has a clear sense that the difference between the civilized and the uncivilized worlds—between seventeenth-century England and the world of contemporary Native Americans, for instance—was political, intellectual, and in a broad sense technological. Machiavelli was skeptical about the value of gunpowder because the Romans had not known of it. Hobbes had no doubt that seventeenth-century men knew a great deal more than their forebears.

The thought that it is not Hobbes but Machiavelli who marks the arrival of modern ways of thinking about politics is by no means foolish. At least two ways of defending it make very good sense. The first is to see Machiavelli as announcing the autonomy of politics as a human activity with its own rules and its own standards of success, standards not drawn from natural law or from an overarching Christian cosmology. On this view, what the classical and the medieval worlds have in common, at least in the works of political philosophers, is a moral and metaphysical framework, within which politics is to be judged by transcendental standards, not by worldly success alone. What Machiavelli insists on is that the political realm is all about acquiring, holding, and using power. Success is a matter of technique, and political analysis is the analysis of these techniques. The second essentially elaborates on this thought, paying less attention to the idea of the autonomy of the political realm, and more to the breach with older notions of mankind's being subject to a natural law that set standards of legitimacy for private as well as public conduct. These ideas have some force, even if it is hard to think of any piece of wickedness that Machiavelli condones when it is necessitated by the demands of either the safety of the state as a whole, or the security of the ruler in particular, that is not also condoned by older writers. The natural law that the Athenians appealed to in answering the Melians was not an overarching moral law in the Christian or the Stoic sense; it was the rule of brutal *raison d'état* that Machiavelli is often credited with having invented. If we should think of Hobbes as marking the birth of modern ways of thinking about politics, and we think that a new view of natural law is part of that, then Hobbes's highly articulate account of the laws of nature and their philosophical status is in a wholly different category from Machiavelli's silent ignoring of such arguments.

LIFE AND TIMES

Thomas Hobbes is the greatest of British political thinkers, and the boldest, most exciting, and most compelling writer on politics in the English language. He is not the best loved or the most sensible; but even his enemies, of whom he had many, acknowledged that he wrote better than all his virtuous opponents put together. It was neither the first nor the last time the devil had the best tunes. Whether Hobbes was surprised by their hostility is anyone's guess. He claimed that anyone who read his work with an unprejudiced mind would be compelled to believe it; the fact that they did not was dismissed with the observation that "when reason is against a man, he will be against reason," which was not calculated to make friends. He was born prematurely on Good Friday, 1588; his mother was frightened by the rumor—unfounded then but true in September—that the Spanish Armada had been sighted in the Channel, and went into labor. "And hereupon my Mother dear, did bring forth twins, both me and fear" was Hobbes's later comment on this beginning, and fear is the passion to rely on as the watchword of his masterpiece, *Leviathan*, published in 1651.[1]

He was born in Malmesbury, Wiltshire, where his

father was a country clergyman, of few intellectual attainments. He had a violent temper; one day he struck a parson at the church door, fled his parish, and died "beyond London."[2] An uncle sent Thomas to the local grammar school and then to Oxford. It was the route for a bright boy with no money. He might become a clergyman or lawyer or the confidential secretary of an aristocrat, or tutor to an aristocrat's son. Of Hobbes's undergraduate career nothing is known, save that he had a taste for snaring birds with pieces of cheese attached to limed string.[3] Later relations with Oxford were bad. He engaged in unedifying debates with Robert Boyle over the possibility of a vacuum, and with John Wallis over the possibility of squaring the circle. The chancellor of the university, the earl of Clarendon, wrote a large volume attacking *Leviathan*, and after Hobbes's death the university condemned his writings and burned them in the quadrangle of the Bodleian Library.[4]

After Oxford he became tutor and chaperone to the son of the earl of Devonshire and, with a break during the civil war, remained with the Cavendish family for the rest of his life. He taught the young man Latin, Greek, mathematics, and history, the accomplishments of a gentleman. He also spent an unconscionable time borrowing money on his master's behalf during their tour of Europe in the 1630s; the downside was waiting in the rain for his money, the upside, spending long hours in other men's libraries, in one of which he read Euclid and fell in love with geometry.[5] Hobbes's first political work was a gift to his employer: a translation of Thucydides's *History of the Peloponnesian War*. He thought it highly relevant to his own times. Thucydides was an effective critic of Athenian democracy, and Hobbes never shed his antipathy to popular government.

Soon afterward, Hobbes changed his mind about the route to political wisdom. Thucydides taught the lessons of history. Hobbes now sought an ahistorical science that would demonstrate from first principles the essence of political authority and what rulers and subjects must do to avoid war and secure peace and prosperity. In 1642, as the civil war was breaking out, a work entitled *The Elements of Law*, which he had written in the previous year, was published without his consent. The book implied that Parliament had no case against the king; Hobbes was terrified that Parliament would imprison or kill him. He fled to France and attached himself to the court of the Prince of Wales, the future Charles II, whose (rather unsuccessful) tutor he was for a time.

The fortunes of the royal and parliamentarian sides ebbed and flowed during the war, and the parliamentarians emerged victorious in 1647. After Charles escaped captivity and tried to recover his throne, he was definitively defeated, tried for treason, and executed on January 30, 1649. To many royalists, this was martyrdom, the blasphemous murder of the Lord's anointed. Hobbes concluded that the royalist game was up and that sensible people must make their peace with the government of Oliver Cromwell. It was then that Hobbes wrote *Leviathan*, which many readers today read as a defense of absolute monarchy, but which was a defense not of *monarchy* but of absolute *authority* in whatever person or persons it was vested. Hobbes certainly thought that monarchy was the best form of government, but he did not think that it was possible to demonstrate it. What he thought he had demonstrated was that political authority must be absolute. The moral of *Leviathan* was that subjects had a duty to obey and assist any regime that would guarantee peace and would allow them to prosper by their own efforts. If Cromwell's protectorate would make peace with him, he would make peace with it. Hobbes had been desperately ill in Paris; he was in his sixties and felt very old; he wanted to go home. When the protectorate offered amnesty and the restoration of property to anyone who would "engage," that is, swear allegiance to the new government, Hobbes went home.

Charles II did not bear him a grudge. At the Restoration in 1660, he invited Hobbes to court and made a pet of his old teacher, who was widely acknowledged to be a considerable wit. But after a few years, Hobbes fell afoul of the church; he was a sharp critic of the pretensions of the clergy, while they thought he corrupted the morals of the court and its hangers-on. His unorthodox opinions made him an easy target, and there was a move to have him tried for heresy. It was an open question whether the medieval statute *De heretico comburendo*—"Of the burning of heretics"—was valid law, but Hobbes, who prided himself on his timidity, did not want to test it. He retired to the country, where he was sheltered by the Devonshires at Chatsworth; he died there in 1679, at the age of ninety-one. It was unkind of the University of Oxford to burn his works as a second best to burning their author, because Hobbes ends *Leviathan* with the hope that his doctrines would be ordered to be taught in the universities "from whence the Preachers, and the Gentry, drawing such water as they find, use to sprinkle the same (both from the Pulpit and in their Conversation) upon the People."[6] Three centuries later, Hobbes is remembered and the time-serving reactionaries who burned his books are not.

THE FIRST POLITICAL SCIENTIST?

Hobbes claimed that the science of politics was no older than himself. Before him, historians and rhetoricians—

Cicero, Machiavelli, or Erasmus—gave advice based on historical evidence, engaged in simple moral exhortation, or showed off their rhetorical skills. Hobbes claimed to be the first to put the understanding of politics on a scientific basis. He thought that the chief obstacle to the creation of a genuine science of politics was the self-interest of Scholastic philosophers, priests and professors, rhetoricians, and obscurantists. His particular bugbears were those who wanted to revive the ancient republics and Roman *libertas* and those who wanted to derive political authority from religion, whether bishops of the Church of England, the pope, or the assorted self-proclaimed prophets who had sprung up during the civil war. To understand Hobbes as he would have wished, we must explore this claim.

Hobbes's life was deeply affected by two revolutions, one the civil war of the 1640s, the other the intellectual revolution associated with Galileo, Descartes, and English scientists such as Robert Hooke, William Harvey, and Robert Boyle. The first led him to think that any society in which there was doubt over the location of authority and its extent was doomed to civil war; if it avoided it, it was only by good luck. *Leviathan* spelled out Hobbes's argument that the unity of a state consisted in the location of an absolute and arbitrary legislative and executive authority in one person or body of persons; the sovereign (who might be one person, several persons, or the entire political community) possessed unlimited legal authority, and subjects were obliged to obey it in everything that did not threaten their lives or require them to deny Christ. Even if they were required to deny Christ, they should do so, trusting God to know what was in their hearts.[7] We should first place *Leviathan* in the context of Hobbes's intellectual allegiances, then very briefly explore Hobbes's idea of "science." The modern reader is apt to be puzzled that Hobbes thought geometry was a science and to wonder what sort of science Hobbes's theory of politics is. Then we can analyze the central argument of *Leviathan*, which takes the reader from a contentious account of human nature through a contentious picture of the state of nature and on to a still more contentious claim about the need to establish a sovereign authority with absolute and arbitrary power to determine and enforce law. Finally, we should notice how Hobbes makes his claims a lot less alarming by reminding us that a prudent government will do much that it is not legally obliged to do, and will not do much that it is legally entitled to do.

Hobbes's intellectual history and allegiances were complex. As a young man he hoped to make his name as a man of letters; his translation of Thucydides's *History of the Peloponnesian War* and his numerous later Latin poems, including a Latin *Autobiography*, are accomplished and vigorous. After his famous encounter with geometry, and his discovery of the new physical science, he became passionate about optics, but also got into academic scrapes and quarrels in which he came out badly, particularly in controversy with Wallis over the squaring of the circle and with Boyle over the possibility of the vacuum.[8] For our purposes, Hobbes's literary achievements and the deficiencies of his understanding of the new physics matter only insofar as they suggest that Hobbes was pitched into becoming a political theorist by events, and that he was telling the truth when he said that he would rather have lived in quiet times and studied optics.

Leviathan is one of the greatest works of political theory ever penned, but it gives a misleading impression of Hobbes's intellectual attachments. *Leviathan* praises political *science* at the expense of what Hobbes calls "prudence."[9] "Prudence" was Hobbes's term for classical statecraft, the attempt to derive maxims of sound political conduct from the analysis of history and the observation of how people behave in difficult situations. It is what Aristotle sometimes, and Thucydides, Polybius, and Machiavelli always, engaged in. Classical statecraft was defended against Hobbes by his contemporary Sir James Harrington, and afterward by David Hume and others. Hobbes was not an unequivocal critic of a politics based on historical analysis and empirical observation. He not only translated Thucydides in 1629 but engaged in some Thucydidean history of his own after the civil war. To *Leviathan* he added *Behemoth*, a little-read volume, to provide what he called "an historical narration" of the civil wars. It is there that he complains that careless readers of the classics have acquired views on tyrannicide that threaten the peace.[10]

Hobbes's ambivalent reactions to historical writing for political purposes had a simple basis. He thought that Thucydides was "the most politic historiographer that ever writ," and agreed with him that democracy was an intrinsically unsound form of government, not least because democracies got into self-destructive wars and were prone to faction and dissension. But history was put to dangerous uses in seventeenth-century England. Republican writers were moved by their reading of history to advocate tyrannicide; others claimed that the lesson of history was that political freedom existed only in popular republics. Most writers other than himself, he thought, were not thinkers; they decorated their political prejudices with historical allusions to show how well-read they were. They allowed rhetoric to substitute for thought. The attack seems paradoxical: *Leviathan* is itself a masterpiece of well-turned rhetoric. That was no accident; rhetoric was acceptable as the servant of reason. If his discovery of the principles of political science was as original as he thought, rhetoric would make his new science more digestible. What made it science, however, was logical cogency, not literary attractiveness.

Hobbes's first political work in his mature style was *The Elements of Law*. He had imagined a longer work, in three portions, inspired by his encounter with Descartes and his circle in Paris during the 1630s when he and his young master were touring Europe. It was to be in Latin and consist of sections on the nature of physical objects (*De corpore*), on man (*De homine*), and on the citizen (*De cive*); in the end, the third section appeared in 1642 in English as *The Elements of Law*, the first and second only in 1655 and 1658. The work that was published as *De cive* in 1642 and 1647 is more nearly a first draft of *Leviathan*. Hobbes feared that his hostility to the pretensions of Parliament might endanger his life, but his skeptical and secular defense of absolute monarchy was as unwelcome to those who believed that Charles I was king by divine right as his assaults on Parliament were to the friends of popular government. His assault on the idea that a state aims at "liberty" for its citizens implied that subjection to law, like all other forms of subjection, including slavery, is simply inconsistent with liberty. Nobody except its author could be happy with that conclusion. *De cive* was written in Latin in 1642, while he was in exile in Paris; an unauthorized English translation appeared in 1647 and caused Hobbes great anxiety. But the one thing

Hobbes could not or would not do to protect himself was to keep quiet.

Whether *Leviathan* was written to ease Hobbes's return to England is moot. Whatever Hobbes's motives, it remains astonishing. Every page contains philosophical insights—or assertions—that repay scrutiny 350 years afterward. Philosophically, the contentious and difficult view that human beings are *no more than* complicated mechanical systems is argued with a mixture of deftness and clumsiness that remains engaging when computer analogies have been commonplace for decades. Hobbes's insistence that sovereignty must be absolute, omnicompetent, indivisible, and ultimate is still fiercely debated, though rarely with reference to Hobbes. His views on the nature of law, the connections of church and state, religious toleration, and much else repay any amount of analysis. Before we engage in it, we should ask what Hobbes's contemporaries made of it.

They understood that *Leviathan* justified Hobbes's submission to the protectorate established by Cromwell. In 1651 Cromwell required subjects who wished to keep their property to "engage" with the new regime, that is, swear allegiance. Only the better-off and politically active had to decide whether or not to swear allegiance, but for them it was a controversial question. Many felt that since they had pledged their allegiance to Charles I they could not go back on their word. Charles was dead and could neither hold them to their allegiance nor release them, but many felt bound to him and his heirs. The question when a man was free to take on new allegiances if not explicitly released by the person to whom he had sworn allegiance before was not easy, but Hobbes provided a clear answer. Once we have pledged allegiance to a government, be it monarchy, aristocracy, or democracy, we are obliged to obey it and help sustain its authority.[11] A sovereign political entity exists to secure the safety of its subjects, and it can do so only if everyone upholds its authority. If in spite of our efforts, the sovereign disintegrates—if the regime is defeated in war or dissolves in civil strife—we may submit to a new sovereign. No sovereign is truly a sovereign who cannot preserve the lives of his subjects. Everyone understood the implication: once Charles I had been defeated in the civil war and could not protect his subjects, they were free to pledge allegiance to whoever could protect them. Others said something similar; Hobbes was unusual in embedding the thought in a complex and comprehensive account of *all* our political rights and obligations.

Many contemporaries fell back on Saint Paul's injunction to "obey the powers that be, for the powers that be are ordained of God," or on the thought that Oliver Cromwell's forces had been victors in a just war, or on an appeal to the right of conquest by which English lawyers had always justified William the Conqueror's right to rule, and the title of his successors. Most people acquiesced in the government of whoever could keep order, were grateful the war was over, and had no need of philosophical assistance. Hobbes wrote for an audience that was used to thinking about its obligations and whose support made a difference to whether the government of the day could govern. They were startled, for instance, by his claim that a man who submits to the conqueror with his sword at his throat submits freely.[12] This was not founding sovereignty on the right of conquest, a familiar move, but founding it on consent, and describing the nature of that consent in highly counterintuitive ways.

LEVIATHAN AND SCIENCE

What Hobbes thought science, and therefore *political* science, was is surprisingly hard to say. What it is not, is easy. It is not Aristotelian. It is not teleological; and it looks behind appearances for the mechanisms that explain appearances. It is decisively post-Galilean. Hobbes draws an analogy with understanding a watch; someone who knows how a watch works can take it to pieces and put it together again. We are to take the state apart *in thought*. The last thing he wanted was that anyone should take the state apart in fact. One might complain that the *mere* ability to take a watch to pieces and reassemble it is no proof of understanding: a good memory might suffice. But Hobbes was interested in the fact that a watchmaker must understand what he dismantles if he is to see what is broken and repair it; a knowledgeable but clumsy horologist might be a poor watch repairer but able to instruct a deft assistant. When Hobbes talks of the "art" by which God creates nature and we create the state, the presumption is that just as geometry tells us how to construct *perfect* circles and rectangles, so the science of state building is the science of the construction of a perfect state. Actual states will deviate from perfection, just as a drawn straight line will deviate from perfect straightness.

Hobbes's science of politics begins with an account of human nature, and Hobbes tells us where we must go for knowledge of it: "*nosce teipsum; read thyself,*" he says.[13] Hobbes goes on to say that once we have read his account of our passions and opinions in *Leviathan*, "the pains left another, will only be to consider, if he find not the same in himself. For this kind of doctrine, admitteth no other demonstration."[14] Hobbes distinguishes very sharply between the *nature* of our desires and aversions and their *objects*. What we desire and avoid varies from one person to another and within one person from one time to another, but the nature of our passions is common to us all.

Modern readers, for whom "science" means the empirical, physical sciences find it hard to know whether Hobbes believes that we have *scientific* knowledge of the physical world. We know that it is God's creation, and that he has the maker's knowledge of it that we have of geometry. What about us? There are three familiar views, none of them easy to identify as Hobbes's own. The first is that our knowledge of the natural world is well-founded opinion. Physics provides natural histories of the physical world; the laws of physics summarize what we know about the world, and provide recipes for making future discoveries. Geometry is different, because it is knowledge of our own constructions, and Hobbes insists that geometry is the only science with which the Creator has seen fit to bless humanity—until Hobbes's science of politics. But when Hobbes lists the various branches of science, he lists knowledge of the natural world among them.[15]

A second possibility is that our knowledge of the natural world is ideally like our knowledge of geometry. There are principles that nature *must* obey. The universe operates according to self-evident principles; the purpose of thought experiments of the kind Galileo recommended was to uncover those principles. Galileo's demonstration that a body in motion would continue in motion forever, contrary to Aristotle's view, involved asking us to imagine a ball rolled down inside a wineglass. It would travel up the other side of the glass to the height it had been released at. If we now imagine the side of the wineglass lowered until it becomes a flat plane, we can see that barring friction, the ball would travel forever, because it would never reach the height from which it had started. QED. Physics shows how the world must work *if* it conforms to the model drawn by the scientist. The model has the irrefutability of geometry; but whether the world *really* conforms to the model is unanswerable.[16]

A third position is one that Hobbes should have liked, but he contradicts it. The difficulty with the first view is that it implies that the universe *might* have operated according to principles quite different from those on which it actually operates. Hobbes agrees. It is God's universe, built as he chose; if he had chosen to build a universe on different principles, nobody could gainsay him. It is not easy to make sense of that view, because we cannot imagine *what* these principles might be. The difficulty with the second view is that one person finds self-evident what another finds counterintuitive; Hobbes's problems with the idea of a vacuum are evidence of that.[17] The third possibility is to argue that there can be only one physics, just as there can be only one geometry; God could not have designed a different universe, any more than Euclid could have drawn up a different geometry. We now know that different geometries are possible; Hobbes did not.

The reason this matters, to Hobbes or his modern readers, is that many of the difficulties of *Leviathan* have their roots in Hobbes's methodological convictions. It is not surprising that his readers found his ideas hard to swallow. *Leviathan* seems to lay down principles for constructing a commonwealth, but these principles are not advice for founders of republics, or for statesmen or insurgents, such as Machiavelli offered in *The Prince* or the *Discourses*. Hobbes rejects Aristotle's claim that politics is the realm of rules of thumb, and we must be content with only as much certainty as the subject matter allows; but Hobbes has also changed the subject. If he were giving practical advice, he would have to be content with "usually," but he rarely offers advice. Perhaps the most overt practical advice is that *Leviathan* should be taught in the universities.[18]

True science is founded, says Hobbes, on "definitions," or "the imposition of names" and the reckoning of the consequences of names. Hobbes makes life harder for himself and the reader by insisting that naming is in one sense arbitrary, but that in a more important sense it is far from arbitrary. *Blau*, *bleu*, and *azzurro* are synonyms of "blue," and as names of a color none is better or worse than the others, if it names the same visual experience. The definitions of "law," "justice," "author-

ity," and so on can be in Latin, Greek, or English, but
if well-chosen, certainty will be achieved, and if ill-
chosen, confusion and contradiction will result.

His purpose is to get us to understand the nature
of sovereign authority, and the nature of law, and the
nature of justice, and he says firmly, "The skill of making and maintaining Commonwealths, consisteth in
certain rules as doth Arithmetic and Geometry; not as
in Tennis-play on practice only."[19] And this appears to
be what he has in mind when he says in the afterword
to *Leviathan* that "the matters in question, are not of
fact, but of right."[20] If we talk about the state as
Hobbes thinks reason requires, we may not manage
everyday life much better, but we shall not plunge into
war because we are talking nonsense. If *Leviathan* has an
ancestor, it is Plato's search in *Republic* and elsewhere for
definitions of justice, knowledge, piety, or courage. Its
intellectual successor is modern economics. Like
geometry, economics works from definitions to conclusions, and abstracts away from most of human life to
illuminate what perfectly rational agents will do in
their market interactions; it is not a merely empirical
account of what most people happen to do but an
account of what we rationally *must* do, supposing our
ends to be as the theory supposes and ourselves to be
fully informed and rational. In the same way, Hobbes
offers a theory of what human beings *must* do if they

are the rational, well-informed, and fearful creatures
he draws for us.

HOBBES ON HUMAN NATURE

So *Leviathan* begins with a highly persuasive account of
human nature and of the role of reason in human life. It
begins with an account of human nature for both official and unofficial reasons. The official reason is that
since a body politic is constructed from individuals, we
must know the nature of the parts to know the nature
of the "artificial man" that we shall build.[21] The unofficial reason is rhetorical; Hobbes paints a picture of the
capacities that human beings possess in virtue of being
self-maintaining physical systems that perceive both
things outside them and their own bodily states, that
feel desires and aversions, and, above all, that think;
then he provides an account of the basic emotions that
drive such creatures and the more complex emotions
that experience and reason create out of these basic
ingredients; by imagining many such creatures placed
in an environment with no rules, no laws, nobody in
authority who is able to make them act in one way
rather than another—the so-called state of nature—he
gives a striking account of the problem to which government possessing absolute authority is the solution. It

is still known to political theorists and sociologists as "the Hobbesian problem of order."

Hobbes begins from the premise that human beings are complex physical systems—natural automata—endowed with sense, reason, and passions. Much of his account of our intellectual capacities is an exasperated commentary on the nonsense of the Schoolmen, the Scholastic philosophers of his own and the previous two centuries. These are old battles, but Hobbes's uncompromising materialism and nominalism is still exciting. Reason is not a divinely implanted source of illumination; it is the capacity to calculate consequences. Its task is to calculate the consequences of names or, in modern terms, to draw logical inferences. Words get their meaning because human beings impose "names" upon experiences they wish to record. The term "red," for instance, gets its meaning by being imposed upon the experience of seeing a red thing to remind us that the experience was like seeing another red thing. This is not a persuasive theory of meaning in general—it is particularly bad on the meaning of words such as "if" or "and"—but it yields results that Hobbes needs. If everything is body, the world contains only particular entities; but late medieval philosophy invented all manner of terms referring to properties of a more or less occult sort. Where names refer to a suspect entity, Hobbes sometimes declares them "unmeaning"; frequently, he makes the very modern move of analyzing them as the name of something else—the name of a name, for instance.[22]

So Hobbes asserts that almost nothing we say about God is really *about God*. To call God "infinitely good" says nothing about how good God is; it says only that human beings cannot say *how* good God is. Calling God infinitely wise and infinitely powerful is acceptable because the term names the intention to honor God. "Infinite" is the name of our inability to set limits; confessing our inability to limit the attributes of God is to honor him or it.[23] This is more skeptical than anything in Aquinas; Hobbes rejects the idea even of analogical talk. What lies beyond all experience is literally inconceivable. This leads to interesting claims: we cannot know whether God wishes us to honor him by praying with our heads covered—as the Jews suppose—or uncovered—as Christians suppose. But we should worship in a way we all recognize as giving honor: bareheaded or with covered heads, however *we* express honor. This has implications for religious liberty and the separation of church and state; on the one hand, it suggests that uniformity of worship is a good thing, on the other, that this is not for "religious" reasons.

Everything in the world is *particular*, and everything universal is verbal; Hobbes is firmly on the materialist, nominalist, and anti-Platonist side in matters of logic.

Traditional philosophy must reduce its ambitions; it cannot see into the essences of things, as Plato hoped. There are no essences. For reason to operate effectively, it must not be dazzled by verbal confusion, whence the need for meticulous definitions, and an end to the unmeaning speech of the Schoolmen. But reasoning is social as well as individual; our opinions can be corrected by other people, and the use of reason implies a willingness to defer to other people. If everyone tries to impose his own ideas on others or to define words as he wants, reasoning is as impossible as playing cards would be if everyone "declared that suit to be trumps of which he had most in his hand." Hobbes is not Humpty Dumpty; words do not mean whatever we want them to mean.[24]

We reason for the sake of successful living. We are moved to do so because we are self-preserving creatures and wish to know how to preserve our lives and how to live well. Hobbes despised Aristotle's ethics and politics. He also despised his physics but conceded some merit to his biology. *Leviathan* was intended to drive Aristotle from the terrain of political debate, but Hobbes silently appropriates his views on many occasions, and our motives for reasoning about the world and ourselves may be one. There is nothing un-Aristotelian about the thought that we are so made that we have a standing desire for self-preservation, and a desire to live well, and that practical reason is the employment of our reason in deciding what to do to secure the good life. If Aristotle's observations are acceptable, the system in which he places them is not. It is absurd and the fount of absurdity. Hobbes's system operates on a mechanical, not a teleological, conception of desire and aversion: something within us drives us to, or away from, what we want or wish to avoid. Our desires are explained by how we are constructed, not by ends inscribed in nature to which we are naturally drawn; the final end of action is set by our desires, not by natural impulsion toward the good. Aristotle's teleological conception of human nature is rejected, and with it any suggestion that we have "proper" or "natural" ends. Aristotle saw values inscribed in nature; Hobbes saw values inscribed on nature by ourselves in the light of our desires and aversions.[25]

GOOD AND EVIL

Hobbes gives a strikingly subjective account of the nature of good and evil and of a vexed subject, the existence of an ultimate good, the summum bonum. He famously observed that "whatsoever every man desireth, that for his part he calleth good." *Good* is not the name of a quality of things or states of affairs; it is the name of our desiring whatever it is. What we dislike, we call evil; and what we are indifferent about, we call, in Hobbes's seventeenth-century terminology, "contemnible." The reality is our wishes and fears; "calling good" is prior to "being good." The things we want, we call good, and happiness consists in getting what we want. This holds only for the most part; many things are wanted as the means to something else, and if they turn out to be wrong or to have bad side effects, so that we are mistaken to want them, we shall not be happy getting what we want. Success consists of satisfying one desire after another; and greater happiness rather than less is the result of satisfying more desires rather than fewer, discounting for side effects. This is a strikingly anti-Aristotelian conclusion, reinforced by another. Aristotle's conception of the ultimate good was associated with the idea that once achieved, it leaves us no further longings. It is ultimate in all ways, embracing all partial goods and leaving the desiring soul in a state of rest. Hobbes was cautious enough about giving offense to the pious to refrain from mocking the thought too savagely. Nonetheless, he dismissed it instantly as a thought without any application to the world we actually live in.[26]

The reason is that we are physical systems. The human body is in incessant motion; our desires are constantly changing, and with them the standard by which we judge our happiness and misery. What Hobbes is careful to call "the felicity of this life"—leaving it unspoken but implicit throughout that we can form no clear idea of what the felicity of any other life may be like—consists in satisfying as many of these changeable desires as we can, one by one. There are "second order" desires—the desire that other desires should be satisfied, and the desire that other people's desires should be satisfied: that is what benevolence is. Among these second-order desires, the desire for security is especially powerful. The traditional doctrine of the common good is silently demolished, although a nontraditional account of a very different common good replaces it. We do not naturally converge on any particular goal: there is nothing that pleases everyone, and nothing satisfies any individual forever. Once a desire is satisfied, another takes its place, and we begin the search to satisfy it. This is not to be deplored; nobody thinks it gluttony to eat lunch as well as breakfast. The felicity of the angels makes no sense to us, though we may hanker after whatever we suppose it to be.

The mutability of desire launches two powerful thoughts. The first is Hobbes's analysis of pride. In the modern vernacular, pride is an extreme version of "keeping up with the Joneses." The changeability of our desires means that the standard of how well we are doing comes from within us; but it cannot answer the question whether we get what we should. What we habitually do is look at how other people are doing. If they do better than we, we envy them; and they envy us if we do better than they. We come to desire their envy, their admiration, and their acknowledgment that we are doing better than they. We move from wanting things "naturally," in the familiar sense of that term, to wanting them because other people want them. We want a bicycle, move on to wanting a car, and end by wanting a car to make the neighbors jealous. "Vainglory" is the most important emotion in Hobbes's political theory; in the Book of Job, Leviathan is "ruler over the children of pride," and Job provides both the title and the moral of Hobbes's masterpiece. *Non est potestas super terram quae comparetur ei*: "there is no power on earth that compares with him." Unsurprisingly, one of Hobbes's innumerable critics entitled his attack on Hobbes *Leviathan Drawn Out with an Hook.* It was nonetheless an unfortunate title, since the implication of God's invocation of the great whale was that Job could not draw it out with a hook. Hobbes regarded pride as a peculiarly antisocial emotion; political arrangements had to subdue it, if there was to be peace.

Pride must yield to its opposite; men must consider their most important, long-term interests and concerns. They must understand that they are fragile creatures for whom self-preservation is the overriding imperative, and think about what behavior promotes self-preservation, not what would impress others. Among consequences disagreeable to traditionally minded aristocrats, two are striking. The first is an insistence on the natural equality of all mankind. There are no natural aristocrats; Aristotle thought exactly the opposite—just as there are slaves by nature, so the "best men" are best by nature. Hobbes insists that what it means to be an aristocrat is a matter of what the sovereign authority determines. The crown is the "fount of honor" in the conventional sense, and in a logically more stringent sense: "honor" is what the sovereign confers. Once the two thoughts are put together, we can see that there is no room in Hobbes's theory for any social group to claim to have a natural right to rule in virtue of birth and upbringing. Hobbes was not hostile to the aristocracy. The Cavendish family employed him for almost six decades, he admired the "aristocratic" virtues, such as generosity, and he had little time for merchants or commercial life. He was hostile not to aristocrats but to the idea that there were any "natural" aristocrats.

The second powerful thought is Hobbes's inversion of Aristotle's search for the summum bonum. There can be no consensus on the highest good for mankind, but there is a worst evil, and that is death. *Everyone* has good reason to avoid "sudden and violent death" at all costs; in the absence of a summum bonum we can agree on the existence of a *summum malum*.[27] That death is the worst of all evils is almost a physical truth for Hobbes; as self-maintaining automata, we are "hard-wired" to reject anything that will bring us to a halt. Hobbes says over and over that we may rationally agree to anything except to get killed. A promise or covenant to kill myself or to let myself be killed is void. This has the curious consequence that the coroner's verdict of suicide while of unsound mind is a pleonasm. To kill oneself appears to be insane by definition. It also has some interestingly liberal results; one is that we cannot say to our rulers, "If I do thus and such, kill me." The most we can say is "If I do thus and such, you may *try to* kill me," with the implication that we do no wrong if we try to ensure they do not. Having established sudden and violent death as the ultimate evil, Hobbes inverts much else of Aristotle's view of politics. We come together to establish a political community not out of a sociable impulse to pursue the good life in common but out of an unsociable fear of one another, and for the sake of avoiding the greatest of all evils, death. Without a state, we have no pleasure but much grief in keeping company.[28]

This is not to say that *once a state is established*, its purpose is exhausted by the protection of life and limb; Hobbes is insistent that the state exists to promote what he calls "commodious living," and commodious living includes all the pleasures and benefits of civilized life, certainly starting with law and order but continuing through economic prosperity and on to the benefits of learning and the pleasures of friendship and sociability. Many of the goods that Aristotle assumes as the *point* of the state's existence reappear as *products* of its creation; but the distinctively political good of ruling and being ruled in turn is not one of them. Hobbes despises the suggestion that the state exists because human beings are naturally sociable, or *political animals*, in the Aristotelian sense. As he says (misrepresenting Aristotle), men are not political creatures as bees or cattle are, coming together by natural impulse; states exist artificially, set up by agreement among individuals with strong views about their own rights and the terms of association. Aristotle pointed out precisely this, but whereas Aristotle thought man was a political animal intended by nature to live in a polis, Hobbes was a thoroughly modern thinker who repudiated the idea that nature had any purposes for us whatever, and emphasized that we were driven into political society. The consequence is that for Hobbes it is no loss if we live wholly private lives and take no interest in politics, while for Aristotle it would be a truncated existence suited to women and slaves but not to citizens.

THE STATE OF NATURE: THE WARRE
OF ALL AGAINST ALL

With this apparatus, and these glimpses of where the argument will go, we can follow Hobbes as he first plunges mankind into the miseries of the state of nature, shows them the way out of those miseries, and elaborates the consequences for a well-constructed and well-conducted state. Men are rational, self-preserving, in touch with the physical world through the medium of the senses. Their language names experiences and allows them to record and anticipate past and future experiences. On these premises Hobbes erects a wholly secular and arm's-length account of religion. The *natural* basis of religion, as distinct from revelation, is that men come to a belief in God through anxiety about causes. We constantly try to discover the cause of events that concern us—the preceding events on which they follow; knowing causes allows us to control events. Following the chain of causes backward, we reach the thought of a cause from which all later events follow, the first cause. This first cause we call God. Belief in God so defined is almost devoid of content, save that it is impossible that we should think any being is capable of creating the universe without also thinking that it is exceedingly—"infinitely"—powerful and has our fate in its hand.[29] Two notable features of Hobbes's discussion are his insistence that religion is a matter of law—"doctrine allowed"—and his constant animadversions against the self-interested overreaching of the priests of the Catholic Church "and even in that church that hath presumed most of reformation."[30]

What of those who disbelieve in the existence of God? Hobbes says they are fools, but not sinners; sin is rebellion against divine law, but those who do not believe in the lawgiver cannot be bound by his laws. God may destroy them as enemies, but he cannot punish them as disobedient subjects. We are "fools" to disbelieve, because it is imprudent to take risks with omnipotence. Hobbes's view that fear is the passion to rely on is not only the observation that a government must be able to frighten the recalcitrant into obedience; it is also the thought that to turn ourselves into law-abiding citizens and morally decent individuals we must look to the roots of law and ethics in our need for security. We are encouraged to see the good sense of being on the safe side in the matter of belief in God.

Mankind in the state of nature has the intellectual capacities of civilized men and is deprived only of government. The state of nature is not a primitive or historical condition; it is a theoretical construct. Among the qualities of natural man, the most important is the desire for *power*. This is not specifically political power. Power in Hobbes's understanding is a label for the capacity to control future events. Our present resources for controlling the future constitute our power. Anxious creatures like ourselves *must* want power; once we have eaten, we wonder where the next meal will come from; we need "power" over the food we shall need in future. I may gather food from the bushes, but only if I can be sure of coming back and not finding them stripped by others can I be sure of my next meal. I need to control the bushes' fate. Hobbes thinks that we move swiftly from power over inanimate things to power over people; what happens depends on what other people do, so controlling them is the key to all control. Control over other people is the core of any account of power.

Hobbes insists that *all* of us have a restless desire for "power upon power that ceaseth only in death." This is not because we are power hungry, or full of immoderate appetites, but because we are driven to acquire power to protect ourselves. It was essential that Hobbes could argue that most individuals were ready to live modestly and have moderate aims in life, and yet that under the wrong conditions they would have to behave *as if* they were power hungry, aggressive, and immoderate. If everyone was power hungry by nature, there would be no hope of establishing government; if nobody cared about his own safety, politics would be unintelligible. Secure people will not seek to dominate others, but insecure people will be forced to try for the sake of survival. And power is essentially comparative; if we both want to exercise control over some part of nature, the one who can make the other yield has the real power. So we are forced to try to acquire more power than others; they are forced to try to acquire more power than us. We are in an arms race, even though we may all wish to escape it. The implications for modern nation-states engaged in literal arms races are very obvious. The sources of power are innumerable: strength, obviously, but riches, wisdom, and honor are all power for Hobbes: whatever allows us to bend other men's wills to our own.

WARRE

In the state of nature, this leads to no good. Hobbes provides a wonderfully mordant account of what he describes as "the natural condition of mankind as touching their felicity," otherwise, "the miseries of life without government," in which he spells out the effect of living in an environment where there are no rules, and no means of enforcement. The problem is not only that there is no authority that can make us behave in one way rather than another; there is also no common judge of right and wrong. Under government we know who owns what, and who can dictate what happens to this money or these goods or this field. Absent that, none of us has any reason to think that he has less right to anything than anyone else has. As Hobbes bleakly says, in these conditions we all have a right to everything, even to the use of one another's bodies. It is a right that nobody can make use of. What we lack is a mechanism for allocating determinate rights that we can make use of. Recall that Hobbes said, "Whatsoever each man desires, that for his part he calleth good." My own survival is a good to me, but perhaps not to you; your paying your debt to me is a good to me, but not to you. We can all understand that *if* there were a common judge who could decide on our rights and duties, we would be better off, inasmuch as we would all be in less danger of sudden and violent death. To get us to fully appreciate that point, Hobbes spells out what we are logically forced to do in the absence of that common judge.

Hobbes says that there are three causes of quarrel—causes of the war of all against all. They are competition, diffidence, and vainglory. Competition is self-explanatory. If we are all anxious about securing the resources on which our survival depends, and there is no mechanism to provide that security, we have to grab what we can, and that can only be at one another's expense. It is equally easy to see how government cures the problem. Under government clear rules about ownership mean we know how lawfully to acquire the means of life. Only in extreme conditions may we be driven to seize what belongs to another lest we starve.

Diffidence or mutual fear is hardly more complicated, but it leads directly into the reasons why twentieth-century international relations theorists "rediscovered" Hobbes after World War II. Hobbes's claim was that the *logic* of interaction between self-interested individuals who can kill one another tends to violence. The argument was reformulated in the twentieth century by mathematically minded strategic theorists. Hobbes's premise is that each individual possesses the ability to injure and, in the last resort, to kill any other human being. The strongest man is vulnerable to the weakest when asleep. Since we all know this, we all have a reason to fear everyone else; the only conditions under which we are safe from another person is if he is disabled from killing us. The most effective way of disabling him is to kill him. Since we are rational, we can calculate that all other persons have a reason to kill us and, in the absence of a deterrent, may do so. That they have a reason to kill us stems from the combination of fear and rationality and the absence of a deterrent. *If* they fear we may kill them, their only recourse is to strike first; there is no government to deter us by threatening us with punishment, nor to deter them. We may have no desire to strike, but we may be forced to do it.

This was the situation in the international sphere when the United States and the Soviet Union possessed enough nuclear weapons to "take out" the other side's weapons, but not enough to survive a first strike with enough weapons to retaliate. Each side had a strong incentive to attack first, however little it might want to in the abstract. "Mutual assured destruction," the alarming name given to the policy of acquiring enough weapons and protecting enough from attack to maintain "second-strike capacity," made both sides safe. Once each side could retaliate, neither had an incentive to launch a first strike. Since each knew that about the other, the motives tending to peace were reinforced. What makes the story relevant is that individuals cannot develop a "private" second-strike capacity. To put it another way, a state with second-strike capacity is not "killed" if it is attacked, because it can retaliate. The individual who is killed cannot retaliate. We need the state to provide us with a second-strike capacity. States do not need a supranational state in the same way, though small states may well form alliances with more powerful states to provide it.

The emphatic rationalism implied by Hobbes's view of science makes all the difference to his argument. If the question whether human beings can survive without government is a simple empirical question, the answer is that in many parts of the world they do, as Hobbes well knew. Rules are accepted and observed by everyone in the absence of formal mechanisms for announcing them and enforcing them. Families and tribes live in hunter-gatherer communities with little formal authority; they do not live very peacefully, but they rarely fall into terminal fratricidal conflict. But no member of such groups would think his life worth a moment's purchase if he found himself among strangers—precisely because they would not acknowledge the rules of forbearance toward him that his family and neighbors would. In essence, members of primitive societies are safe where family-level sanctions work, and unsafe where they do not. Hobbes wants to show us the implications of removing government from our own society, which is to say the kind of society that had experienced the English Civil War of the 1640s. It was not a society where the family-level forbearances and sanctions of a primitive society would suffice.

The final reason for conflict is not on all fours with competition and diffidence. Competition can be assuaged by prosperity when we can earn a living by hard work and intelligence. And our willingness to seek our living that way rather than by violence is much increased by the existence of law and its enforcement. Fear may be reduced almost to nothing when we all know that everyone else has every reason *not* to assault us. Pride is different. We have seen how pride results from the combination of the instability of our desires with the ability to compare our successes with those of others; it is the source of an unremitting urge to "come top," no matter what the competition is about. In any competition there is only one top place, and competition for it cannot be diluted by prosperity. Pride makes men overestimate their capacities and take foolish risks; it leads men to be obstinate when they would preserve the peace by being willing to give in gracefully. It leads them to seek occasions to increase the resentment felt by their competitors, when peace suggests we should soothe their feelings. The cures for pride are twofold. The first is that the sovereign is understood to be the fount of honor, and that all understand their social status to be in the sovereign's gift. The other is simply to repress its expression as far as possible. *Leviathan* is king over the children of pride.

THE LAWS OF NATURE

When competition, diffidence, and vainglory drive us into conflict, it is no wonder that Hobbes supposed that life in the state of nature would be "poore, solitary, nasty, brutish, and short." This does not impugn human nature, and our actions are not sinful. Unlike Machiavelli, who says bleakly that men are evil and will do all the evil they can, Hobbes thinks they are essentially innocent. They are frightened of sudden and violent death and must do whatever they can to avoid it. In the wrong conditions, that makes things worse rather than better. The sense in which Hobbes is an Augustinian about politics does not extend to sharing Augustine's obsession with original sin. The same emotions and intelligence that lead to the war of all against all can secure peace and prosperity under stable and orderly government. We reach that conclusion in two steps. First, we must ask what will bring about peace. Hobbes has no doubt that everyone will agree that we need rules to make us keep the peace and fulfill our agreements with one another. The answer to the question "What rules would we do well to follow?" is the "laws of nature."

Unlike his predecessors, Hobbes says that they are not strictly *laws*. Strictly speaking, laws are commands issued by an authority entitled to issue such commands: "the word of him that by right hath command over others."[31] The laws of nature are "theorems" about what "conduces to the safety of them all." As theorems, they are not rules but conclusions about rules within a piece of hypothetical reasoning—"*if* we all followed the injunction to keep our covenants, peace and prosperity would ensue," and so on. A command is an imperative: "keep faith, practice justice, eschew cruelty," and the like. Hobbes thinks of the rules of morality, which is what the laws of nature are, as imperatives we address to ourselves. We may choose to think of them as the laws of God, in which case they are properly laws, divine laws. They are always binding on the conscience, which is to say we should always *wish* to act on them and be willing to do so when it is safe, but we are not bound to act on them unless it is safe to do so. Hobbes marks the distinction as between being obliged *in foro interno* and *in foro externo*.

The basis of the laws of nature is the preservation of mankind. It was an old thought that God created the world with a view to its preservation; his laws were intended to preserve the creatures whom he had created. Hobbes does not diverge very far from that perspective in spite of his methodological originality. The first law of nature commands us to seek peace; the corollary is that where peace is not to be had we may use all the helps and advantages of war. The first clause is the first law; the second clause, the first right. Hobbes is unclear about how the laws of nature achieve their end. He begins by saying they are precepts found out by reason whereby a man is forbidden to do what is destructive of his life. This is plausible in the sense that *if* everyone else obeys the rules, we shall do well to obey them. But if others do *not* follow the rules, following them is dangerous since others will take advantage of us. The rules are good for us collectively if we all obey them; for an individual thinking selfishly, what matters is whether others obey them. Selfishly, I need others to keep the peace, keep promises, and behave decently. Purely selfishly, I do best if they keep the rules and I do what I choose. The literary expression of that thought goes back to Callicles and Thrasymachus, and more credibly to Glaucon.

Hobbes never raises this anxiety, what is today known as the free-rider problem. The explanation is probably that he did not think that we are selfish *in that sense.* We are *"self-*ish" in the sense that if any of us has an aim it must be *ours;* I can take your pain seriously only if your pain distresses *me,* just as I can take seriously the fact that you are relying on my promise only if honesty matters to *me.* This thought is easily confused with the view that I take my promise seriously only instrumentally—that I keep my promise only to get something on a later occasion from you or from others who notice my honesty. They are not the same thought. Hobbes did not think that we are all selfish in the derogatory sense; some of us are and some of us are not. All of us are self-centered in a physical or physiological sense that is wholly consistent with being benevolent, honest, and just. Our desires are the psychological manifestation of a physical system that attempts (implausibly as a matter of physiology) to maximize the flow of vital motions about the heart (equally implausibly described as being what we feel as happiness). It is a necessary truth that we do what leads to our happiness. It is not a truth at all that we cannot be made happy by being honest, honorable, and benevolent.

OBLIGATION

Like many previous thinkers, Hobbes explains earthly authority, which is to say the sovereign's right to command, in terms that imply both an ascending and a descending view of authority. God's authority is another matter entirely; God can command us because he created us and does not need our assent to be able to make us act as he wishes. Earthly sovereigns are created by the consents of their subjects. What distinguishes Hobbes from his predecessors is his obsessive attention to the individual subject. Where Justinian claimed that "the people" conferred absolute authority on him, Hobbes is concerned with our obligation to obey the sovereign's commands, and he finds that obligation in our individual consent.[32] The question is one not of the pedigree of an existing sovereign but of the moral obligation of each individual. The politically central laws of nature are the second and third. The second tells one to be willing to lay down the right to all things "and to be contented with so much liberty against other men as he would allow other men against himself." The means of laying down our rights is to contract or covenant with others for the purpose; the third law of nature therefore dictates "that men perform their covenants made." Justice consists in fulfilling our obligations; obligations are imposed by us on ourselves when we make a contract or covenant.

Hobbes thought that injustice was literally illogical. One can see why he might have done so: to say, "I promise that I will do such and such, but I have no intention of doing so," comes very close to saying, "I shall and I shall not do it." Hobbes's argument does not achieve what is wanted; *saying* "I promise" while having no intention to do it is not self-contradictory but wicked. The contradiction between what I say and what I know I shall do is, as with lying, the essence of deceit but not a defect of logic. It certainly undermines the possibility of good order; *pacta servanda sunt*—"promises must be kept"—is as important as everyone from Cicero onward has maintained. And it is certainly true that just as communication would be impossible unless most of us most of the time said what we thought to be true, so the institution of promising would simply not exist unless most of us most of the time took the obligations we

assumed as seriously as we should. The greater problem
for Hobbes's system is this. Hobbes intends that in the
state of nature we make a covenant "of all with all" to
establish government, that is, to create the artificial
body we call the sovereign. But, say many of his critics,
he tells us that covenants in the state of nature do not
oblige, so the covenant cannot oblige.

This is wrong. Hobbes held two views that are in
tension but not at odds. Covenants always oblige *in foro
interno*, which is to say that we must be willing to do
what we have promised, if it is safe to do it. In the state
of nature we are thrown back on our own judgment
about what we must do to preserve ourselves; this is the
effect of the absence of government. It might seem that
we can always find a reason to weasel out of what we
have promised. Once there is government, obeying the
rules is safe, and there is agreement on what excuses will
or will not hold water; so finding excuses not to perform becomes impossible. But Hobbes never says that
in the state of nature the laws of nature do not oblige;
he claims they do "not always" oblige *in foro externo*. That
implies that they sometimes, perhaps often, do oblige.
The first law of nature obliges always; it demands only
that we seek peace, and no matter what the difficulties,
we can always do that. The second law of nature, which
requires us to be willing to give up our rights on condition that others give up theirs on equal terms, is equally

easy to obey. It is not difficult to be *willing* to consent on equal terms to the creation of government; the difficulty lies in actually laying down my right if that exposes me to attack by others.

The laws of nature, then, oblige always in intention; they bind us to promote peace. They are not *conditional*; they do not invite us to observe them if we wish, or when we think they are to our advantage. We need not observe them *in foro externo* if it is too dangerous; but we are not at liberty to ignore them as we choose. This is essential for the next step of the escape from the state of war. The escape depends on our contracting with one another; Hobbes's account of contract or covenant is the key to everything that follows. Hobbes claimed that although we are obliged to obey the laws of nature *as laws* if they are thought of as the laws of God, the obligation to obey human law rests on our prior agreement to obey a human lawgiver. Nobody is under an earthly obligation that he has not placed himself under; *injustice* consists of a breach of such obligation. Two powerful consequences are that nothing the sovereign does can be unjust, in Hobbes's sense; and that our obligations to the governments we live under have been freely undertaken by ourselves.[33] It is worth recalling yet again that this is not a historical story about the genesis of government; Hobbes says that was a matter of families becoming clans and clans becoming kingdoms. *Leviathan* is an account of right, not fact.

SOVEREIGNTY

The covenant that takes us out of the state of nature is a covenant of every man with every man to transfer all their rights to "this man or this body of men," and to take his or their word as *law*. This *institutes* a sovereign. The sovereign is an artificial body—recall the frontispiece of *Leviathan*—and as an artificial person it represents us all, and we are the authors of its acts. Hobbes devotes a lot of detailed explanation to this point, as he needs to do in order to bring off a claim that looks very like squaring the circle. Previous writers who defended absolute monarchy agreed that in extremis kings who were excessively unjust and had therefore become tyrants might be desposed. Hobbes claimed that the sovereign could not commit injustice, because its acts are literally ours. This was not to say that whoever bears the sovereignty cannot behave badly; he might perpetrate *iniquity* and violate the laws of nature and of God. Strictly speaking, however, he could not act unjustly, a point Hobbes reinforces by insisting that it should be unlawful to talk about tyranny at all, no doubt thinking that from discussing the nature of tyranny it would be a short step to advocating tyrannicide. Hobbes's attention to the institution of the sovereign is justified. Although almost all sovereigns in fact acquire authority over their subjects by *acquisition*, institution underlies the existence of all sovereigns. Hobbes understood this and acknowledged that there is a sense in which democracy underpins even absolute monarchy, that sense is that there is no legal system unless all (or the vast majority) accept its requirements as obligatory.

The details of Hobbes's account of the sovereign's institution excite curiosity and skepticism. Critics have wondered why Hobbes said that covenants without the sword are but words and of no power to hold a man at all, and yet relied on a covenant without the sword to create the sovereign who was to wield the sword. *Once* the covenant establishing the sovereign has been entered into, it is maintained by the sword of the sovereign; the difficulty is reaching that point. It is crucial to Hobbes that the sword does not create the obligation imposed by the covenant; I create the obligation that binds me when I covenant. The role of the sword—that is, the sovereign's power to compel me—is to remove any excuse for nonperformance. *I* am bound by my agreement; *you* are bound by your agreement. You may wonder whether I will meet my obligations if no external power can make me do so; I may wonder the same about you. If we are each ready to meet our obligations, the knowledge that there is a sword to ensure that the *other* party performs removes the excuse to not do what we are willing to do. The sword can remain in its sheath;

its bare existence achieves what is needed. Second, what sustains government is the readiness of the citizenry to support it—so long as it is not too dangerous. That is a moral, not a legal, commitment. And that is what the covenant of all with all amounts to.

Hobbes was preoccupied with the thought that *one* person or body of persons must be sovereign, that is, to be the unique source of law in a political community. If there is to be obedience to law, we must know what the law is; someone must have the last word on that. Hobbes regarded theories of divided sovereignty as disastrous, and this was a popular refrain among defenders of absolute monarchy. The thought that we might settle on a person or group as the focus of obedience and obey them because everyone else obeys them is not implausible, nor is the argument that if it is to be the source of ultimate authority here on earth, it must be absolute at least in the sense of owning no superior and having no *legal* constraints on what it can do. It opens the door to a thought common in writers of a republican persuasion, but entirely alien to Hobbes. In the republican tradition, the founders of states play a special role. How a state *begins* is decisive for its future health and longevity, and the founding father or fathers correspondingly important. Hobbes has no time for such questions. He is explaining what a state is, and what underpins the claim of a sovereign to absolute authority; its longevity hinges not on its origins but on everyone who matters understanding what a commonwealth is, and what that means for his obligation to support it. The thought that underlying our "vertical" allegiance to this or that ruler—Charles I or Cromwell—there must be a horizontal allegiance to our fellow citizens is a decidedly modern and egalitarian thought. *Perhaps* it is true in fact that creating a state depends on finding a charismatic founder; but what is true in logic is that unless we have some one source of authority entitled to lay down the law and enforce it, we have no state at all, only anarchy.[34]

Hobbes envisaged two sorts of sovereign, although the attention he bestowed on them was in inverse proportion to their occurrence in the world. The *sovereign by institution* is the sovereign authority created out of the state of nature, while the *sovereign by acquisition* is an existent sovereign acquiring new subjects. The second case covers the silent, continuous acquisition of new subjects that takes place as young people become old enough for their allegiance to concern an existing government. It also covers—more importantly for Hobbes—the case where persons defeated in war are spared on condition of subjecting themselves to a new ruler. Making the leap from the state of nature into the political condition is the more intellectually demanding matter; but Hobbes lavished equal ingenuity on both.

The sovereign by acquisition offers the person who may or may not become a subject a simple choice: "obedience or death." Hobbes argued that in this case a promise extorted by force is valid; what normally invalidates the promise to pay a substantial sum the next day to the highwayman who offers you "your money or your life" is the fact that his activity is legally prohibited, and the justified fear that he will kill you if you turn up. The sovereign can spare your life very easily; when he has done, he has fulfilled his side of the bargain, leaving you no excuse not to fulfill yours. Hobbes insisted that the bargain is made "freely." His argument that a promise made out of fear is binding is not wholly unpersuasive. We do not think that a customer who buys bread from a baker need not pay his bill just because he was afraid of going hungry. Why should we think a defeated enemy is excused from obeying his captor just because he was anxious not to be killed? Fear of privation and fear of death are equally fear of coming to a nasty end. In fact, Hobbes tries to be too clever. Many conditions make bargains more or less coercive and therefore less or more binding. The situation when there is one baker in town, famine threatens, and the baker offers to feed us only if we become his slaves is very different from the usual situation where there are many bakers, and the worst that happens if we do not like his bread or his prices is a walk to another baker. The sovereign by acquisition is in the first situation rather than the second.

The claim to which all this is preamble is that the *sovereign* is not bound by any promise to his or their subjects. Hobbes had nothing but contempt for theories of mixed government, and for those who thought that a king's coronation oath constituted the sort of promise that someone else might legitimately try to enforce. It is essential to Hobbes's theory that we give up *all* the rights we can transfer to the sovereign. We cannot give up the right to save our own lives in extremis, so there is no point in trying. All other rights are transferred. The sovereign by institution is not bound by this covenant, because we covenant with one another and not with the sovereign. The sovereign by acquisition is not under an obligation to us, because he fulfilled his side of the bargain when he spared our lives, and has no further obligation to us. Hobbes took a strikingly individualistic view about obligation. We are under an obligation to obey our rulers because we have put ourselves under that obligation. Unlike traditionalists and conservatives, Hobbes did not think we are born into obedience. Most people assent silently to the government in power in the society into which they are born, but in logic the sovereign might legitimately treat them as "enemies" until they explicitly engage to obey him. The sovereign's forbearance is to be understood as the terms for obedience.

Having elaborated the nature of sovereignty and its intellectual origins, Hobbes went on to give an account of the powers and duties of sovereigns and of the nature of life under law. That account has many peculiarities, but its main feature is not a peculiarity but central to accounts of sovereignty for the next several centuries. The point of the sovereign's existence is to settle the question of what the law is in some particular jurisdiction. What the sovereign commands as law is law. The sovereign's laws may be well judged or ill judged, but what makes them laws is not their goodness but their being commanded as rules to guide those subject to them. This is a "pedigree" theory of law, because it claims that the way to discover whether a purported law is really a law is to see whether it has been laid down in the right way by the appropriate authority. For this to be possible, Hobbes thought, the sovereign must be one, indivisible, and absolute. The reason is obvious enough; a decisive answer to the question of what the law is requires an authority able to answer that question. There can be only one such authority, since if there were more than one they might give conflicting answers. The existence of the United States of America suggests other possibilities: one of which is that a sovereign is not what Hobbes says—since the United

States possesses a multiplicity of legal systems and no single final arbiter of conflict; or, that the possession of an identifiable sovereign is not a necessary condition of being a single state—since the United States is a single political system, but different bodies have the last word on different issues.

Hobbes had no doubt that divided sovereignty was disastrous. But once he had defended absolute authority as essential to a state's existence, he gave an account of how a state should in fact be governed that made so many concessions to constitutionalist ideas that many commentators have described Hobbes as a "protoliberal," if not a liberal. The awkwardness is that most liberals think citizens have rights against their governments; such as a right to free speech, to the free practice of whatever religion seems compelling to them, to the immunities against arbitrary arrest and ill-treatment we see enshrined in bills of rights. Hobbes, however, insisted that subjects have no such rights. The natural rights we are born with are useless in the state of nature; we give them all up—except the right to save our lives in extremis— to create the government that will protect us.

We have no right to free speech; there is no "right to private judgment," such as Protestant dissenters claimed; there is no right to be represented. The king's ministers are counselors; they do not share sovereignty and have

no right to have their advice accepted. Hobbes agreed
that political bodies should act by majority decision, but
had no enthusiasm for democracy as a political system.
A body must speak with one voice, and how else to
determine that one voice but by majority decision?
Hobbes was unequivocally unliberal if liberalism is a
matter of individual rights. His hostility to "free institutions" was unflinching. The city of Lucca wrote the
word "Libertas" in great letters on its walls. But nobody
could claim that a citizen of Lucca was freer—that is,
had more immunity from the service of the commonwealth—than an Ottoman in Constantinople.[35] Freedom under government consists "in the silence of the
laws";[36] a relaxed absolutism left the citizenry freer than
an austere republicanism.

Hobbes's employment of this conception of freedom opens the door to another, non-rights-based form
of liberalism. It rests on a negative conception of liberty; freedom is *not* being made to act in one way rather
than another. The protoliberal element in Hobbes was
his conviction that although governments are *entitled* to
legislate on anything whatever, they should actually
enact as few laws as possible. The reasoning is what one
might expect. What constitutionalists demand from
government as a matter of *right* are generally good things
in themselves. Governments that consult widely legislate more intelligently; governments that avoid legislat-

ing over the minute details of life have happier, and therefore more loyal, subjects; if religion is not likely to cause dissension if left to individual discretion, governments should allow everyone to choose her or his own religious allegiance, at any rate within much the limits that Locke later set out. But peace trumps everything. Where religion is contentious, a compelled uniformity of worship and public doctrine is necessary. The liberal who talks of rights might agree to abrogate the *right to free exercise of religion* in emergency; Hobbes would regret that "independency" was impossible.

Hobbes argues that rulers should behave as if a liberal, constitutional order were in place on instrumental grounds. It is not necessary for the government to legislate us into work and trade; we want to be prosperous and do not need governments to make us do it. What we need is two forms of assistance: first, protection against force and fraud, so that we are not hesitant to take risks because we fear to be robbed or deceived; second, helpful commercial laws. Force and fraud aside, the great handicap to prosperity is unclear laws about ownership and contract. Hobbes advocated an English land register in 1651; it was created only when Parliament finally passed the Real Property Act of 1925. Laws about ownership and contract are minimally coercive; they do not oblige anyone to own anything or make a contract with anyone. They offer individuals the assistance of the state's coercive powers when certain conditions are fulfilled; if you and I make a valid agreement, we can each have it enforced against the other. If we make invalid agreements, we are mugs. Hobbes was not, in fact, an enthusiast for trade, employment, or commercial life in general. He had an intellectual's tastes, not a merchant's. But he believed very firmly that government exists first to keep the peace and then to promote all the arts of civilization, commercial and intellectual.

The small touches that display Hobbes's concern to avoid misery above all else include his advocacy of a (minimal) welfare state. The old, the poor, and the unemployed needed help, and a prosperous society should provide it. This is further evidence that Hobbes's view of human selfishness was not the view that we are doomed to think only of ourselves and to promote only our own interests; if we were so doomed, no society would be possible. There is no difficulty in Hobbes's suggestion that we should provide for the poor, the old, and the sick; we are not so selfish that benevolence toward them is impossible. John Aubrey tells a nice story to make the point that the fact that our feelings of sympathy must be *ours* does not mean they are not feelings of sympathy. "One time I remember going in the Strand, a poor and infirme old man craved his alms. He, beholding him with eyes of pity and compassion, put his hand in his pocket and gave him sixpence. Said a Divine that stood by, 'Would you have done this if it had not been Christ's command?'" Hobbes's answer was spot-on: "I was in pain to apprehend the miserable condition of the old man, and now my alms giving him some relief doth also relieve me."[37] The same concern to avoid pointless misery animates Hobbes's discussion of religious toleration. Almost half of *Leviathan* is devoted to the topic of a "Christian Commonwealth"; after Hobbes had taken his readers from human nature through the state of nature, thence through the principles of all government whatever, he had to tackle the subject that passionately animated his contemporaries—the politics of a Christian society.

THE CHRISTIAN COMMONWEALTH

From the point of view both of modern commentators and Hobbes's historical legacy, there is a certain awkwardness in the lengthy discussion of "The Christian Commonwealth." In Western societies, churches go out of their way to disavow secular political ambitions, so Hobbes's modern readers are not as interested in the subject as his contemporaries were. They were used to religious zealots arguing that the classical doctrine of tyrannicide justified the assassination of a heretical

monarch, and to other enthusiasts advocating the institution of the kingdom of God on earth at the first
opportunity. The argumentative Hobbes also felt honor
bound to fight off many current theological views and
to defend some unorthodox views of his own. He was,
for instance, a "mortalist," which is to say that he
believed that at death we perish entirely, without continuing to exist as an immortal soul; at the Last Judgment, we shall be created anew and judged; the righteous
will be granted eternal, bodily existence, and the
unrighteous will be annihilated. Hell as the resting
place for the damned vanishes from the story. Mortalism was not uncommon, though disapproved of. Today
it is a historical curiosity. What presents even more difficulty is the fact that if one imagines Hobbes posing
the question what difference it makes to a commonwealth that it is a Christian commonwealth, his reply is
that it makes none. This is not as astonishing as it
might seem, but it has an interesting consequence.

Hobbes argued that religion grew out of anxiety.[38]
The human mind is driven to search for the causes of
the things that affect our lives; reaching backward along
the chain of causes, we finally think that there *must* be
some uncaused cause of the sequence, and that we call
God. We saw, too, that Hobbes held that "natural the-
ology" was all but a contradiction in terms; unaided
reason could tell us nothing about the nature of God,

save that he exists and is more powerful than we can set limits to. That skepticism allowed Hobbes to insist that religion is more important as social practice than as intellectual speculation, and must be regulated in the way any other social practice must be regulated—with a view to preserving the peace and physical and psychological security.

Among obvious threats to the peace are self-proclaimed prophets claiming to have a new revelation of God's intentions. Hobbes maintained that prophets ceased when God ceased to provide them with miraculous powers; nowadays, the proper view is that when a man says that God spoke to him in a dream, we should understand that he dreamed that God spoke to him. Hobbes did not deny that Jehovah revealed himself to his chosen people; he merely argued that that fact put the Israelites in a unique situation, which was that until they chose kings for themselves, God was their earthly sovereign. Once he allowed them to choose an earthly sovereign for themselves, God continued to rule the earth in the sense that all believers were obliged to obey his commands, but he was not an earthly sovereign. Anyone attempting to set up a godly kingdom on English soil would rightly be jailed.

As to doctrine, orthodoxy was for the sovereign to define. A sensible sovereign would avoid causing his people anxiety by requiring them to profess beliefs that

stretched credulity or came into conflict with their
other beliefs; that was asking a man to play at cross and
pile for his salvation and frustrated the purpose of government. In any case, men can and may dissimulate in
such matters, and a wise sovereign contents himself
with outward conformity. Toleration within limits
enters through the back door. As to the sacred books of
the Christian tradition, the Bible receives its authority
from the sovereign. Hobbes had mixed views about the
translation of the Bible into English; it gave anyone who
could read a compendious account of their duties to
man and God, but it also encouraged people to publish
strange interpretations of God's word. They must
remember that it is an essential attribute of sovereignty
that the sovereign alone may decide what doctrines may
lawfully be taught.

A Christian commonwealth thus turns out to be
one in which the sovereign's authority over doctrine
extends to authority over Christian churches. Hobbes's
aim was to secure the priority of state over church and
to ensure not merely that wild men from the country-
side did not set up as prophets but that bishops did not
arrogate secular authority to themselves. The bishops
would have burned Hobbes as a heretic if the chance
had come their way, so mutual animosity was not surprising. There was one area where Hobbes was unsure
of his step. This was the ancient problem of the duty of

a Christian subject to obey an infidel sovereign. Hobbes insisted that no subject had the right to challenge the legitimacy of a sovereign on religious grounds, and it was easy to see that Christians must in general obey infidel rulers to the point where they demand that we deny Christ. In *De cive*, Hobbes held that at this point the devout must refuse and "go to Christ" by martyrdom. He changed his mind in *Leviathan* and argued that we could deny Christ to save our lives. God enjoined us to preserve ourselves and would not regard the denial as a mortal sin. What a man says and what is in his heart are two different things, and God is concerned with what is in our hearts. His concern, evident in the immensely long chapter 42 ("Ecclesiastical Power"), is to insist that there is no "spiritual power" independent of, separate from, and differently founded from the secular power. There are not two swords, but one. The sovereign wields both sword and scepter.

CONCLUSION

We therefore find Hobbes arguing consistently for a state whose authority is unlimited, but which exercises that authority discreetly. Since religion was the great source of contention in the seventeenth century, it was the authority of the state over the church that he was particularly anxious to defend, but in the hope that it will be exercised with a light touch. Arguing against Bishop Bramhall over free will and necessity, Hobbes insisted that religion is a question of law, not truth, which is what he consistently argues in *Leviathan*. Philosophical speculation is one thing, the expressive and moral functions of religion another. How far this was religious skepticism is impossible to say. The range of religious opinion in the sixteenth and seventeenth centuries was wide; none of Hobbes's far-fetched interpretations of the Bible were unique to him, and mortalism in particular was a common view of the afterlife. We may think it casts a curious light on the Last Judgment that dead persons are re-created to be judged for sins that an earlier version of themselves committed in the distant past; but that may well have seemed easier to believe than that disembodied souls existed. We may wonder whether Hobbes's materialism allows room for God, at all; his critics insisted that it did not and that he was an atheist, but Hobbes does not appear to have thought it a problem.

That leaves us with one last riddle. Hobbes thought he had rendered it only "probable" that absolute monarchy was the best of all forms of government; but he was sure that he had proved beyond question that government must have absolute authority, that a constitution could not be sovereign, and that divided authority was disastrous. Later critics were unkind. Locke asked why men who feared to be attacked by polecats should think themselves safer to be the potential prey of lions. Hobbes believed that a rational monarch would see that his interests were identical with those of his subjects. If they were happy and prosperous, they would obey his government and support it conscientiously. Hobbes insisted that we are obliged to support that power by which our safety is secured, which implies the possibility of a "virtuous" (as distinct from a vicious) spiral, where successful government breeds loyalty, which breeds successful government, which breeds . . . The rational sovereign will read *Leviathan* and understand that a temperate government that secures the livelihoods of the citizenry, does not encroach upon their privacy, and encourages initiative, imagination, art, and science will create a loyal, intelligent, and adventurous population.

The difficulty comes with a less intelligent or less competent sovereign, whether this is one man carried away by whim, pride, or ambition or an assembly riven by discord. What can we do? Hobbes had no answer. So much did he fear that his fellow subjects were looking for every least excuse to avoid their duty that he weighted the scales against self-help to an absurd degree. He agrees that we may resist the sovereign *on our own behalf alone* if we are directly threatened; since self-protection is hard-wired into the human organism, nothing we do can commit us to allowing the sovereign to kill us without resisting. Hobbes thought this implied that the sovereign should not add to the penalties of the criminal law further penalties for evading detection or trying to escape the agents of the law. But Hobbes's difficulty is that by insisting that we may resist only to save our own lives and only on our own behalf, he contradicts his own account of human nature and renders resistance too difficult. Anxious creatures gathering evidence about what danger they may be in can hardly help taking the way the sovereign treats others as evidence about how he might treat us. If we see that the sovereign seems bent on folly or misrule, we can scarcely avoid thinking it might be better to hang together than to hang separately, and form an alliance to resist the irrational sovereign while we can. Luther had in essence faced the issue and evaded it by acknowledging that a ruler who behaved badly enough would find that his subjects ignored the Pauline injunction to obey the powers that be and overthrew him, rightly or wrongly. The subjects of a Hobbesian sovereign cannot help asking whether the sovereign may turn from protecting them to attacking them. If the latter, the sovereign and they are back in the state of nature, and they may use all the helps and advantages of war. Hobbes's only recourse is to urge us to give the sovereign the benefit of the doubt, and to urge the sovereign to recall that his or their glory rests on the prosperity and happiness of their subjects.

Nonetheless, the only *authority* over the sovereign is that of conscience and God. It is not difficult to see that, faced with so few resources of our own to oppose to those of the sovereign, subjects might reasonably feel either that they do not care whether it is technically an error to describe the sovereign as unjust—"iniquitous" is the proper term—so long as they can say they are justified in rebellion when the sovereign gets out of hand, or that they are happy to run the risk that divided government will collapse in chaos, seeing that as between a regime of checks and balances on the one hand and the Hobbesian sovereign on the other, it is a question of which presents the lesser evil. To none of this does Hobbes have a conclusive response. It is unfair to suggest that he should have had one. His achievement was to draw a more compelling picture of the political predicament than anyone before him, and one that has never been bettered. The considerations that tell for and against confiding more or less authority to government, and drawing the bands of obedience tighter or looser about the subject, have never been better set out. That his readers, and we ourselves, must make up their own minds about where the balance should finally be struck is a fact of political life, not a failure in Hobbes.

NOTES

1. Hobbes, "The Verse Life," in *Human Nature and De Corpore Politico*, ed. J. C. A. Gaskin (Oxford: Oxford University Press, 2008), p. 224.

2. *Aubrey's Brief Lives*, ed. J. A. K. Thomson (Harmondsworth: Penguin Classics, 1959), p. 148.

3. Ibid., 149.

4. Henry Hyde, earl of Clarendon, *A Brief View and Survey of the Dangerous and Pernicious Errors to Church and State, in Mr Hobbes's Book Entitled Leviathan* (Oxford, 1676); R. A. Beddard, "Tory Oxford," in Nicholas Tyacke, ed., *Seventeenth-Century Oxford*, vol. 4 of *The History of the University of Oxford* (Oxford: Clarendon Press, 1997), p. 897.

5. *Aubrey's Brief Lives*, p. 150.

6. Hobbes, "A Review and Conclusion," *Leviathan*, ed. Richard Tuck (Cambridge: Cambridge University Press, 1991), pp. 707–8.

7. Hobbes, *Leviathan*, p. 344.

8. Steven Shapin and Simon Schaffer, *Leviathan and the Air-Pump: Hobbes, Boyle, and the Experimental Life* (Princeton: Princeton University Press, 1989), recounts the arguments with Boyle.

9. Hobbes, *Leviathan*, p. 117.

10. Hobbes, *Behemoth*, ed. Stephen Holmes (Chicago: University of Chicago Press, 1990), p. 3.

11. Hobbes, *Leviathan*, p. 718.

12. Ibid., p. 252.

13. Ibid., p. 82.

14. Ibid., p. 83.

15. Ibid., pp. 147–49.

16. Ibid., pp. 147–48.

17. Shapin and Schaffer, *Leviathan and the Air-Pump.*

18. Hobbes, "Review and Conclusion," p. 727.

19. Ibid.

20. Ibid.

21. Hobbes, *Leviathan*, pp. 80–82.

22. Ibid., p. 107.

23. Ibid., p. 171.

24. Ibid., pp. 111–12.

25. Ibid., p. 120.

26. Ibid., pp. 129–30.

27. Ibid.

28. Ibid., p. 185.

29. Ibid., pp. 168–70.

30. Ibid., p. 183.

31. Ibid., p. 217.

32. Emphasized in "Review and Conclusion," pp. 718–21.

33. Hobbes, *Leviathan*, pp. 251–52.

34. Ibid., pp. 228ff.

35. Ibid., p. 266.

36. Ibid., p. 271.

37. *Aubrey's Brief Lives*, p. 157.

38. Hobbes, *Leviathan*, p. 169.

Selections

A NOTE ON THE SELECTIONS

TEACHERS OF POLITICAL THOUGHT usually take students through chapters 13 to 21 of *Leviathan*, and this is substantially what the following extracts cover. Before chapter 13, Hobbes develops his account of human nature, including an account of speech, language, and science, as well as an account of our passions—hopes and fears. But he provides in chapter 12 a rather deflationary account of the natural origins of religion, which I have included here, together with its natural companion, his account of God's kingdom by nature in chapter 31. To convey an impression of Hobbes's talent for offensive humor, I have included a few pages of chapter 47, in which he savages the papacy and the Catholic priesthood. It is worth noting that chapter 31 also concludes with Hobbes's summary of what he has achieved in the first two books of *Leviathan* and his hope that a well-disposed sovereign might turn it into doctrine to be taught to his people.

LEVIATHAN

INTRODUCTION

NATURE, the art whereby God hath made and governs the world, is by the art of man, as in many other things, so in this also imitated, that it can make an artificial animal. For seeing life is but a motion of limbs, the beginning whereof is in some principal part within; why may we not say, that all automata (engines that move themselves by springs and wheels as doth a watch) have an artificial life? For what is the heart, but a spring; and the nerves, but so many strings; and the joints, but so many wheels, giving motion to the whole body, such as was intended by the artificer? Art goes yet further, imitating that rational and most excellent work of nature, man. For by art is created that great LEVIATHAN called a COMMONWEALTH, or STATE, in Latin CIVITAS, which is but an artificial man; though of greater stature and strength than the natural, for whose protection and defence it was intended; and in which the sovereignty is an artificial soul, as giving life and motion to the whole body; the magistrates, and other officers of judicature and execution, artificial joints; reward and punishment, by which fastened to the seat of the sovereignty every joint and member is moved to perform his duty, are the nerves, that do the same in the body natural; the wealth and riches of all the particular members, are the strength; *salus populi*, the people's safety, its business; counsellors, by whom all things needful for it to know are suggested unto it, are the memory; equity, and laws, an artificial reason and will; concord, health; sedition, sickness; and civil war, death. Lastly, the pacts and covenants, by which the parts of this body politic were at first made, set together, and united, resemble that fiat, or the let us make man, pronounced by God in the creation.

To describe the nature of this artificial man, I will consider

First, the matter thereof, and the artificer; both which is man.

Secondly, how, and by what covenants it is made; what are the rights and just power or authority of a sovereign; and what it is that preserveth or dissolveth it.

Thirdly, what is a Christian commonwealth.

Lastly, what is the kingdom of darkness.

Concerning the first, there is a saying much usurped of late, that wisdom is acquired, not by reading of books, but of men. Consequently whereunto, those persons, that for the most part can give no other proof of being wise, take great delight to show what they think they have read in men, by uncharitable censures of one another behind their backs. But there is another saying not of late understood, by which they might learn truly to read one another, if they would take the pains; that is, *nosce teipsum*, read thyself: which was not meant, as it is now used, to countenance, either the barbarous state of men in power, towards their inferiors; or to encourage men of low degree, to a saucy behaviour towards their betters; but to teach us, that for the similitude of the thoughts and passions of one man, to the thoughts and passions of another, whosoever looketh into himself, and considereth what he doth, when he does think, opine, reason, hope, fear, &c. and upon what grounds; he shall thereby read and know, what are the thoughts and passions of all other men upon the like occasions. I say the similitude of passions, which are the same in all men, desire, fear, hope, &c; not the similitude of the objects of the passions, which are the things desired, feared, hoped, &c: for these the constitution individual, and particular education, do so vary, and they are so easy to be kept from our knowledge, that the characters of man's heart, blotted and confounded as they are with dissembling, lying, counterfeiting, and erroneous doctrines, are legible only to him that searcheth hearts. And though by men's actions we do discover their design sometimes; yet to do it without comparing them with our own, and distinguishing all circumstances, by which the case may come to be altered, is to decypher without a key, and be for the most part deceived, by too much trust, or by too much diffidence; as he that reads, is himself a good or evil man.

But let one man read another by his actions never so perfectly, it serves him only with his acquaintance, which are but few. He that is to govern a whole nation, must read in himself, not this or that particular man; but mankind: which though it be hard to do, harder than to learn any language or science; yet when I shall have set down my own reading orderly, and perspicuously, the pains left another, will be only to consider, if he also find not the same in himself. For this kind of doctrine admitteth no other demonstration.

CHAPTER XII

OF RELIGION

RELIGION IN MAN ONLY.

Seeing there are no signs, nor fruit of religion, but in man only; there it no cause to doubt, but that the seed of religion, is also only in man; and consisteth in some peculiar quality, or at least in some eminent degree thereof, not to be found in any other living creatures.

FIRST, FROM HIS DESIRE OF KNOWING CAUSES.

And first, it is peculiar to the nature of man, to be inquisitive into the causes of the events they see, some more, some less; but all men so much, as to be curious in the search of the causes of their own good and evil fortune.

FROM THE CONSIDERATION OF THE BEGINNING OF THINGS.

Secondly, upon the sight of anything that hath a beginning, to think also it had a cause, which determined the same to begin, then when it did, rather than sooner or later.

FROM HIS OBSERVATION OF THE SEQUEL OF THINGS.

Thirdly, whereas there is no other felicity of beasts, but the enjoying of their quotidian food, ease, and lusts; as having little or no foresight of the time to come, for want of observation, and memory of the order, consequence, and dependence of the things they see; man observeth how one event hath been produced by another; and remembereth in them antecedence and consequence; and when he cannot assure himself of the true causes of things, (for the causes of good and evil fortune for the most part are invisible), he supposes causes of them, either such as his own fancy suggesteth; or trusteth the authority of other men, such as he thinks to be his friends, and wiser than himself.

THE NATURAL CAUSE OF RELIGION, THE
ANXIETY OF THE TIME TO COME.

The two first, make anxiety. For being assured that
there be causes of all things that have arrived hitherto,
or shall arrive hereafter; it is impossible for a man, who
continually endeavoureth to secure himself against the
evil he fears, and procure the good he desireth, not to be
in a perpetual solicitude of the time to come; so that
every man, especially those that are over provident, are
in a state like to that of Prometheus. For as Prometheus,
which interpreted, is, the prudent man, was bound to
the hill Caucasus, a place of large prospect, where, an
eagle feeding on his liver, devoured in the day, as much
as was repaired in the night: so that man, which looks
too far before him, in the care of future time, hath his
heart all the day long, gnawed on by fear of death, pov-
erty, or other calamity; and has no repose, nor pause of
his anxiety, but in sleep.

WHICH MAKES THEM FEAR THE POWER OF INVISIBLE THINGS.

This perpetual fear, always accompanying mankind in
the ignorance of causes, as it were in the dark, must
needs have for object something. And therefore when
there is nothing to be seen, there is nothing to accuse,
either of their good, or evil fortune, but some power, or
agent invisible: in which sense perhaps it was, that some
of the old poets said, that the gods were at first created

by human fear: which spoken of the gods, that is to say, of the many gods of the Gentiles, is very true. But the acknowledging of one God, eternal, infinite, and omnipotent, may more easily be derived, from the desire men have to know the causes of natural bodies, and their several virtues, and operations; than from the fear of what was to befall them in time to come. For he that from any effect he seeth come to pass, should reason to the next and immediate cause thereof, and from thence to the cause of that cause, and plunge himself profoundly in the pursuit of causes; shall at last come to this, that there must be, as even the heathen philosophers confessed, one first mover; that is, a first, and an eternal cause of all things; which is that which men mean by the name of God: and all this without thought of their fortune; the solicitude whereof, both inclines to fear, and hinders them from the search of the causes of other things; and thereby gives occasion of feigning of as many gods, as there be men that feign them.

AND SUPPOSE THEM INCORPOREAL.

And for the matter, or substance of the invisible agents, so fancied; they could not by natural cogitation, fall upon any other conceit, but that it was the same with that of the soul of man; and that the soul of man, was of the same substance, with that which appeareth in a dream, to one that sleepeth; or in a looking-glass, to one

that is awake; which, men not knowing that such appa-
ritions are nothing else but creatures of the fancy, think
to be real, and external substances; and therefore call
them ghosts; as the Latins called them *imagines*, and
umbræ; and thought them spirits, that is, thin aerial bodies; and those invisible agents, which they feared, to be
like them; save that they appear, and vanish when they
please. But the opinion that such spirits were incorporeal, or immaterial, could never enter into the mind of
any man by nature; because, though men may put
together words of contradictory signification, as spirit,
and incorporeal; yet they can never have the imagination of any thing answering to them: and therefore, men
that by their own meditation, arrive to the acknowledgment of one infinite, omnipotent, and eternal God,
chose rather to confess he is incomprehensible, and
above their understanding, than to define his nature by
spirit incorporeal, and then confess their definition to
be unintelligible: or if they give him such a title, it is not
dogmatically, with intention to make the divine nature
understood; but piously, to honour him with attributes,
of significations, as remote as they can from the gross-
ness of bodies visible.

BUT KNOW NOT THE WAY HOW THEY EFFECT ANYTHING.
Then, for the way by which they think these invisible
agents wrought their effects; that is to say, what imme-

diate causes they used, in bringing things to pass, men that know not what it is that we call causing, that is, almost all men, have no other rule to guess by, but by observing, and remembering what they have seen to precede the like effect at some other time, or times before, without seeing between the antecedent and subsequent event, any dependence or connexion at all: and therefore from the like things past, they expect the like things to come; and hope for good or evil luck, superstitiously, from things that have no part at all in the causing of it: as the Athenians did for their war at Lepanto, demand another Phormio; the Pompeian faction for their war in Africa, another Scipio; and others have done in divers other occasions since. In like manner they attribute their fortune to a stander by, to a lucky or unlucky place, to words spoken, especially if the name of God be amongst them; as charming and conjuring, the liturgy of witches; insomuch as to believe, they have power to turn a stone into bread, bread into a man, or any thing into any thing.

But honour them as they honour men.

Thirdly, for the worship which naturally men exhibit to powers invisible, it can be no other, but such expressions of their reverence, as they would use towards men; gifts, petitions, thanks, submission of body, considerate addresses, sober behaviour, premeditated words, swearing, that is, assuring one another of their promises, by invoking them. Beyond that reason suggesteth nothing; but leaves them either to rest there; or for further ceremonies, to rely on those they believe to be wiser than themselves.

AND ATTRIBUTE TO THEM ALL EXTRAORDINARY EVENTS.

Lastly, concerning how these invisible powers declare to men the things which shall hereafter come to pass, especially concerning their good or evil fortune in general, or good or ill success in any particular undertaking, men are naturally at a stand; save that using to conjecture of the time to come, by the time past, they are very apt, not only to take casual things, after one or two encounters, for prognostics of the like encounter ever after, but also to believe the like prognostics from other men, of whom they have once conceived a good opinion.

FOUR THINGS, NATURAL SEEDS OF RELIGION.

And in these four things, opinion of ghosts, ignorance of second causes, devotion towards what men fear, and taking of things casual for prognostics, consisteth the natural seed of religion; which by reason of the different fancies, judgments, and passions of several men, hath grown up into ceremonies so different, that those which are used by one man, are for the most part ridiculous to another.

MADE DIFFERENT BY CULTURE.

For these seeds have received culture from two sorts of men. One sort have been they, that have nourished, and ordered them, according to their own invention. The other have done it, by God's commandment, and direction: but both sorts have done it, with a purpose to make those men that relied on them, the more apt to obedience, laws, peace, charity, and civil society. So that the religion of the former sort, is a part of human politics; and teacheth part of the duty which earthly kings require of their subjects. And the religion of the latter sort is divine politics; and containeth precepts to those that have yielded themselves subjects in the kingdom of God. Of the former sort, were all the founders of common-wealths, and the law-givers of the Gentiles: of the latter sort, were Abraham, Moses, and our blessed Saviour; by whom have been derived unto us the laws of the kingdom of God.

THE ABSURD OPINION OF GENTILISM.

And for that part of religion, which consisteth in opinions concerning the nature of powers invisible, there is almost nothing that has a name, that has not been esteemed amongst the Gentiles, in one place or another, a god, or devil; or by their poets feigned to be inanimated, inhabited, or possessed by some spirit or other.

The unformed matter of the world, was a god, by the name of Chaos.

The heaven, the ocean, the planets, the fire, the earth, the winds, were so many gods.

Men, women, a bird, a crocodile, a calf, a dog, a snake, an onion, a leek, were deified. Besides that, they filled almost all places, with spirits called demons: the plains, with Pan, and Panises, or Satyrs; the woods, with Fawns, and Nymphs; the sea, with Tritons, and other Nymphs; every river, and fountain, with a ghost of his name, and with Nymphs; every house with its Lares, or familiars; every man with his Genius; hell with ghosts, and spiritual officers, as Charon, Cerberus, and the Furies; and in the night time, all places with larvæ, lemures, ghosts of men deceased, and a whole kingdom of fairies and bugbears. They have also ascribed divinity, and built temples to meer accidents, and qualities; such as are time, night, day, peace, concord, love, contention, virtue, honour, health, rust, fever, and the like; which when they prayed for, or against, they prayed to, as if there were ghosts of those names hanging over their heads, and letting fall, or withholding that good, or evil, for, or against which they prayed. They invoked also their own wit, by the name of Muses; their own igno-rance, by the name of Fortune; their own lusts by the name of Cupid; their own rage, by the name of Furies; their own privy members, by the name of Priapus; and attributed their pollutions, to Incubi, and Succubæ: insomuch as there was nothing, which a poet could introduce as a person in his poem, which they did not make either a god, or a devil.

The same authors of the religion of the Gentiles, observing the second ground for religion, which is men's ignorance of causes; and thereby their aptness to attribute their fortune to causes, on which there was no dependence at all apparent, took occasion to obtrude on their ignorance, instead of second causes, a kind of second and ministerial gods; ascribing the cause of fecundity, to Venus; the cause of arts, to Apollo; of subtlety and craft, to Mercury; of tempests and storms, to Æolus; and of other effects, to other gods; insomuch as there was amongst the heathen almost as great variety of gods, as of business.

And to the worship, which naturally men conceived fit to be used towards their gods, namely, oblations, prayers, thanks, and the rest formerly named; the same legislators of the Gentiles have added their images, both in picture, and sculpture; that the more ignorant sort, that is to say, the most part or generality of the people, thinking the gods for whose representation they were made, were really included, and as it were housed within them, might so much the more stand in fear of them: and endowed them with lands, and houses, and officers, and revenues, set apart from all other human uses; that is, consecrated, and made holy to those their idols; as caverns, groves, woods, mountains, and whole islands; and have attributed to them, not only the shapes, some of men, some of beasts, some of monsters; but also the faculties, and passions of men and beasts: as sense, speech, sex, lust, generation, and this not only by mixing one with another, to propagate the kind of gods; but also by mixing with men, and women, to beget mongrel gods, and but inmates of heaven, as Bacchus, Hercules, and others; besides anger, revenge, and other passions of living creatures, and the actions proceeding from them, as fraud, theft, adultery, sodomy, and any vice that may be taken for an effect of power, or a cause of pleasure; and all such vices, as amongst men are taken to be against law, rather than against honour.

Lastly, to the prognostics of time to come; which are naturally, but conjectures upon experience of time past; and supernaturally, divine revelation; the same authors of the religion of the Gentiles, partly upon pretended experience, partly upon pretended revelation, have added innumerable other superstitious ways of divination; and made men believe they should find their fortunes, sometimes in the ambiguous or senseless answers of the priests at Delphi, Delos, Ammon, and other famous oracles; which answers, were made ambiguous by design, to own the event both ways; or absurd, by the intoxicating vapour of the place, which is very frequent in sulphurous caverns: sometimes in the leaves of the Sybils; of whose prophecies, like those perhaps of Nostradamus (for the fragments now extant seem to be the invention of later times), there were some books in reputation in the time of the Roman republic: sometimes in the insignificant speeches of madmen, supposed to be possessed with a divine spirit, which possession they called enthusiasm; and these kinds of foretelling events, were accounted theomancy, or prophecy: sometimes in the aspect of the stars at their nativity; which was called horoscopy, and esteemed a part of judiciary astrology: sometimes in their own hopes and fears, called thumomancy, or presage: sometimes in the prediction of witches, that pretended conference with the dead; which is called necromancy, conjuring, and witchcraft; and is but juggling and confederate knavery: sometimes in the casual flight, or feeding of birds; called augury: sometimes in the entrails of a sacrificed beast; which was aruspicina: sometimes in dreams: sometimes in croaking of ravens, or chattering of birds: sometimes in the lineaments of the face; which was called metoposcopy; or by palmistry in the lines of the hand; in casual words, called omina: sometimes in monsters, or unusual accidents; as eclipses, comets, rare meteors, earthquakes, inundations, uncouth births, and the like, which they called *portenta*, and *ostenta*, because they thought them to portend, or foreshow some great calamity to come; sometimes, in mere lottery, as cross and pile; counting holes in a sieve; dipping of verses in Homer, and Virgil; and innumerable other such vain conceits. So easy are men to be drawn to believe any thing, from such men as have gotten credit with them; and can with gentleness, and dexterity, take hold of their fear, and ignorance.

THE DESIGNS OF THE AUTHORS OF
THE RELIGION OF THE HEATHEN.

And therefore the first founders, and legislators of commonwealths among the Gentiles, whose ends were only to keep the people in obedience, and peace, have in all places taken care; first, to imprint in their minds a belief, that those precepts which they gave concerning religion, might not be thought to proceed from their own device, but from the dictates of some god, or other spirit; or else that they themselves were of a higher nature than mere mortals, that their laws might the more easily be received: so Numa Pompilius pretended to receive the ceremonies he instituted amongst the Romans, from the nymph Egeria: and the first king and founder of the kingdom of Peru, pretended himself and his wife to be the children of the Sun; and Mahomet, to set up his new religion, pretended to have conferences with the Holy Ghost, in form of a dove. Secondly, they have had a care, to make it believed, that the same things were displeasing to the

gods, which were forbidden by the laws. Thirdly, to prescribe ceremonies, supplications, sacrifices, and festivals,
by which they were to believe, the anger of the gods
might be appeased; and that ill success in war, great con-
tagions of sickness, earthquakes, and each man's private
misery, came from the anger of the gods, and their anger
from the neglect of their worship, or the forgetting, or
mistaking some point of the ceremonies required. And
though amongst the ancient Romans, men were not forbidden to deny, that which in the poets is written of the
pains, and pleasures after this life: which divers of great
authority, and gravity in that state have in their harangues
openly derided; yet that belief was always more cher-
ished, than the contrary.

And by these, and such other institutions, they
obtained in order to their end, which was the peace of
the commonwealth, that the common people in their
misfortunes, laying the fault on neglect, or error in their
ceremonies, or on their own disobedience to the laws,
were the less apt to mutiny against their governors; and
being entertained with the pomp, and pastime of festivals, and public games, made in honour of the gods,
needed nothing else but bread to keep them from dis-
content, murmuring, and commotion against the state.
And therefore the Romans, that had conquered the
greatest part of the then known world, made no scruple
of tolerating any religion whatsoever in the city of Rome

itself; unless it had something in it, that could not consist with their civil government; nor do we read, that
any religion was there forbidden, but that of the Jews;
who, being the peculiar kingdom of God, thought it
unlawful to acknowledge subjection to any mortal king
or state whatsoever. And thus you see how the religion
of the Gentiles was a part of their policy.

THE TRUE RELIGION AND THE LAWS
OF GOD'S KINGDOM THE SAME.

But where God himself, by supernatural revelation,
planted religion; there he also made to himself a peculiar kingdom: and gave laws, not only of behaviour
towards himself, but also towards one another; and
thereby in the kingdom of God, the policy, and laws
civil, are a part of religion; and therefore the distinction
of temporal, and spiritual domination, hath there no
place. It is true, that God is king of all the earth: yet
may he be king of a peculiar, and chosen nation. For
there is no more incongruity therein, than that he that
hath the general command of the whole army, should
have withal a peculiar regiment, or company of his own.
God is king of all the earth by his power: but of his
chosen people, he is king by covenant. But to speak
more largely of the kingdom of God, both by nature,
and covenant, I have in the following discourse assigned
another place (chapter XXXV).

The causes of change in religion.

From the propagation of religion, it is not hard to understand the causes of the resolution of the same into its first seeds, or principles; which are only an opinion of a deity, and powers invisible, and supernatural; that can never be so abolished out of human nature, but that new religions may again be made to spring out of them, by the culture of such men, as for such purpose are in reputation.

For seeing all formed religion, is founded at first, upon the faith which a multitude hath in some one person, whom they believe not only to be a wise man, and to labour to procure their happiness, but also to be a holy man, to whom God himself vouchsafeth to declare his will supernaturally; it followeth necessarily, when they that have the government of religion, shall come to have either the wisdom of those men, their sincerity, or their love suspected; or when they shall be unable to show any probable token of divine revelation; that the religion which they desire to uphold, must be suspected likewise; and, without the fear of the civil sword, contradicted and rejected.

Enjoining belief of impossibilities.

That which taketh away the reputation of wisdom, in him that formeth a religion, or addeth to it when it is already formed, is the enjoining of a belief of contradictories: for both parts of a contradiction cannot possibly be true: and therefore to enjoin the belief of them, is an argument of ignorance; which detects the author in that; and discredits him in all things else he shall propound as from revelation supernatural: which revelation a man may indeed have of many things above, but of nothing against natural reason.

DOING CONTRARY TO THE RELIGION THEY ESTABLISH.

That which taketh away the reputation of sincerity, is the doing or saying of such things, as appear to be signs, that what they require other men to believe, is not believed by themselves; all which doings, or sayings are therefore called scandalous, because they be stumbling blocks, that make men to fall in the way of religion; as injustice, cruelty, profaneness, avarice, and luxury. For who can believe, that he that doth ordinarily such actions as proceed from any of these roots, believeth there is any such invisible power to be feared, as he affrighteth other men withal, for lesser faults?

That which taketh away the reputation of love, is the being detected of private ends: as when the belief they require of others, conduceth or seemeth to conduce to the acquiring of dominion, riches, dignity, or secure pleasure, to themselves only, or specially. For that which men reap benefit by to themselves, they are thought to do for their own sakes, and not for love of others.

Want of the testimony of miracles.

Lastly, the testimony that men can render of divine calling, can be no other, than the operation of miracles; or true prophecy, which also is a miracle; or extraordinary felicity. And therefore, to those points of religion, which have been received from them that did such miracles; those that are added by such, as approve not their calling by some miracle, obtain no greater belief, than what the custom and laws of the places, in which they be educated, have wrought into them. For as in natural things, men of judgment require natural signs, and arguments; so in supernatural things, they require signs supernatural, which are miracles, before they consent inwardly, and from their hearts.

All which causes of the weakening of men's faith, do manifestly appear in the examples following. First, we have the example of the children of Israel; who when Moses, that had approved his calling to them by miracles, and by the happy conduct of them out of Egypt, was absent but forty days, revolted from the worship of the true God, recommended to them by him; and setting up (Exod. xxxiii. I, 2) a golden calf for their god, relapsed into the idolatry of the Egyptians; from whom they had been so lately delivered. And again, after Moses, Aaron, Joshua, and that generation which had seen the great works of God in Israel, (Judges ii. II) were dead; another generation arose, and served Baal. So that miracles failing, faith also failed.

Again, when the sons of Samuel, (I Sam. viii. 3) being constituted by their father judges in Bersabee, received bribes, and judged unjustly, the people of Israel refused any more to have God to be their king, in other manner than he was king of other people; and therefore cried out to Samuel, to chose them a king after the manner of the nations. So that justice failing, faith also failed: insomuch, as they deposed their God, from reigning over them.

And whereas in the planting of Christian religion, the oracles ceased in all parts of the Roman empire, and the number of Christians increased wonderfully every day, and in every place, by the preaching of the Apostles, and Evangelists; a great part of that success, may reasonably be attributed, to the contempt, into which the priests of the Gentiles of that time, had brought themselves, by their uncleanness, avarice, and juggling between princes. Also the religion of the church of Rome, was partly, for the same cause abolished in England, and many other parts of Christendom; insomuch, as the failing of virtue in the pastors, maketh faith fail in the people: and partly from bringing of the philosophy, and doctrine of Aristotle into religion, by the Schoolmen; from whence there arose so many contradictions, and absurdities, as brought the clergy into a reputation both of ignorance, and of fraudulent intention; and inclined people to revolt from them, either against the will of their own princes, as in France and Holland; or with their will, as in England.

Lastly, amongst the points by the church of Rome declared necessary for salvation, there be so many, manifestly to the advantage of the Pope, and of his spiritual subjects, residing in the territories of other Christian princes, that were it not for the mutual emulation of those princes, they might without war, or trouble, exclude all foreign authority, as easily as it has been excluded in England. For who is there that does not see, to whose benefit it conduceth, to have it believed, that a king hath not his authority from Christ, unless a bishop crown him? That a king, if he be a priest, cannot marry? That whether a prince be born in lawful marriage, or not, must be judged by authority from Rome? That subjects may be freed from their allegiance, if by the court of Rome, the king be judged an heretic? That a king, as Chilperic of France, may be deposed by a pope, as Pope Zachary, for no cause; and his kingdom given to one of his subjects? That the clergy and regulars, in what country soever, shall be exempt from the jurisdiction of their king in cases criminal? Or who does not see, to whose profit redound the fees of private masses, and vales of purgatory; with other signs of private interest, enough to mortify the most lively faith, if, as I said, the civil magistrate, and custom did not more sustain it, than any opinion they have of the sanctity, wisdom, or probity of their teachers? So that I may attribute all the changes of religion in the world, to one and the same cause; and that is, unpleasing priests; and those not only amongst Catholics, but even in that church that hath presumed most of reformation.

CHAPTER XIII

OF THE NATURAL CONDITION OF MANKIND AS
CONCERNING THEIR FELICITY, AND MISERY

Men by nature equal.

Nature hath made men so equal, in the faculties of the body, and mind; as that though there be found one man sometimes manifestly stronger in body, or of quicker mind than another; yet when all is reckoned together, the difference between man, and man, is not so considerable, as that one man can thereupon claim to himself any benefit, to which another may not pretend, as well as he. For as to the strength of body, the weakest has strength enough to kill the strongest, either by secret machination, or by confederacy with others, that are in the same danger with himself.

And as to the faculties of the mind, setting aside the arts grounded upon words, and especially that skill of proceeding upon general, and infallible rules, called sci-

ence; which very few have, and but in few things; as
being not a native faculty, born with us; nor attained, as
prudence, while we look after somewhat else, I find yet
a greater equality amongst men, than that of strength.
For prudence, is but experience; which equal time,
equally bestows on all men, in those things they equally
apply themselves unto. That which may perhaps make
such equality incredible, is but a vain conceit of one's
own wisdom, which almost all men think they have in
a greater degree, than the vulgar; that is, than all men
but themselves, and a few others, whom by fame, or for
concurring with themselves, they approve. For such is
the nature of men, that howsoever they may acknowledge many others to be more witty, or more eloquent, or
more learned; yet they will hardly believe there be many
so wise as themselves; for they see their own wit at hand,
and other men's at a distance. But this proveth rather
that men are in that point equal, than unequal. For
there is not ordinarily a greater sign of the equal distribution of any thing, than that every man is contented
with his share.

FROM EQUALITY PROCEEDS DIFFIDENCE.

From this equality of ability, ariseth equality of hope in
the attaining of our ends. And therefore if any two men
desire the same thing, which nevertheless they cannot

both enjoy, they become enemies; and in the way to their end, which is principally their own conservation, and sometimes their delectation only, endeavour to destroy, or subdue one another. And from hence it comes to pass, that where an invader hath no more to fear, than another man's single power; if one plant, sow, build, or possess a convenient seat, others may probably be expected to come prepared with forces united, to dispossess, and deprive him, not only of the fruit of his labour, but also of his life, or liberty. And the invader again is in the like danger of another.

From diffidence war.

And from this diffidence of one another, there is no way for any man to secure himself, so reasonable, as anticipation; that is, by force, or wiles, to master the persons of all men he can, so long, till he see no other power great enough to endanger him: and this is no more than his own conservation requireth, and is generally allowed. Also because there be some, that taking pleasure in contemplating their own power in the acts of conquest, which they pursue farther than their security requires; if others, that otherwise would be glad to be at ease within modest bounds, should not by invasion increase their power, they would not be able, long time, by standing only on their defence, to subsist. And by consequence, such augmentation of dominion over men being necessary to a man's conservation, it ought to be allowed him.

Again, men have no pleasure, but on the contrary a great deal of grief, in keeping company, where there is no power able to over-awe them all. For every man looketh that his companion should value him, at the same rate he sets upon himself: and upon all signs of contempt, or undervaluing, naturally endeavours, as far as he dares, (which amongst them that have no common power to keep them in quiet, is far enough to make them destroy each other), to extort a greater value from his contemners, by damage; and from others, by the example.

So that in the nature of man, we find three principal causes of quarrel. First, competition; secondly, diffidence; thirdly, glory.

The first, maketh men invade for gain; the second, for safety; and the third, for reputation. The first use violence, to make themselves masters of other men's persons, wives, children, and cattle; the second, to defend them; the third, for trifles, as a word, a smile, a different opinion, and any other sign of undervalue, either direct in their persons, or by reflection in their kindred, their friends, their nation, their profession, or their name.

OUT OF CIVIL STATES, THERE IS ALWAYS WAR OF EVERY ONE AGAINST EVERY ONE.

Hereby it is manifest, that during the time men live without a common power to keep them all in awe, they are in that condition which is called war; and such a war, as is of every man, against every man. For war, consisteth not in battle only, or the act of fighting; but in a tract of time, wherein the will to contend by battle is sufficiently known: and therefore the notion of time, is to be considered in the nature of war; as it is in the nature of weather. For as the nature of foul weather, lieth not in a shower or two of rain; but in an inclination thereto of many days together: so the nature of war, consisteth not in actual fighting; but in the known disposition thereto, during all the time there is no assurance to the contrary. All other time is peace.

THE INCOMMODITIES OF SUCH A WAR.

Whatsoever therefore is consequent to a time of war, where every man is enemy to every man; the same is consequent to the time, wherein men live without other security, than what their own strength, and their own invention shall furnish them withal. In such condition, there is no place for industry; because the fruit thereof is uncertain: and consequently no culture of the earth;

no navigation, nor use of the commodities that may be imported by sea; no commodious building; no instruments of moving, and removing, such things as require much force; no knowledge of the face of the earth; no account of time; no arts; no letters; no society; and which is worst of all, continual fear, and danger of violent death; and the life of man, solitary, poor, nasty, brutish, and short.

It may seem strange to some man, that has not well weighed these things; that nature should thus dissociate, and render men apt to invade, and destroy one another: and he may therefore, not trusting to this inference, made from the passions, desire perhaps to have the same confirmed by experience. Let him therefore consider with himself, when taking a journey, he arms himself, and seeks to go well accompanied; when going to sleep, he locks his doors; when even in his house he locks his chests; and this when he knows there be laws, and public officers, armed, to revenge all injuries shall be done him; what opinion he has of his fellow-subjects, when he rides armed; of his fellow citizens, when he locks his doors; and of his children, and servants, when he locks his chests. Does he not there as much accuse mankind by his actions, as I do by my words? But neither of us accuse man's nature in it. The desires, and other passions of man, are in themselves no sin. No more are the actions, that proceed from those passions, till they know a law that forbids them: which till laws be made they cannot know: nor can any law be made, till they have agreed upon the person that shall make it.

It may peradventure be thought, there was never such a time, nor condition of war as this; and I believe it was never generally so, over all the world: but there are many places, where they live so now. For the savage people in many places of America, except the government of small families, the concord whereof dependeth on natural lust, have no government at all; and live at this day in that brutish manner, as I said before. Howsoever, it may be perceived what manner of life there would be, where there were no common power to fear, by the manner of life, which men that have formerly lived under a peaceful government, use to degenerate into, in a civil war.

But though there had never been any time, wherein particular men were in a condition of war one against another; yet in all times, kings, and persons of sovereign authority, because of their independency, are in continual jealousies, and in the state and posture of gladiators; having their weapons pointing, and their eyes fixed on one another; that is, their forts, garrisons, and guns upon the frontiers of their kingdoms; and continual spies upon their neighbours; which is a posture of war. But because they uphold thereby, the industry of their subjects; there does not follow from it, that misery, which accompanies the liberty of particular men.

IN SUCH A WAR NOTHING IS UNJUST.

To this war of every man, against every man, this also is consequent; that nothing can be unjust. The notions of right and wrong, justice and injustice have there no place. Where there is no common power, there is no law: where no law, no injustice. Force, and fraud, are in war the two cardinal virtues. Justice, and injustice are none of the faculties neither of the body, nor mind. If they were, they might be in a man that were alone in the world, as well as his senses, and passions. They are qualities, that relate to men in society, not in solitude. It is consequent also to the same condition, that there be no propriety, no dominion, no mine and thine distinct; but only that to be every man's, that he can get; and for so long, as he can keep it. And thus much for the ill condition, which man by mere nature is actually placed in; though with a possibility to come out of it, consisting partly in the passions, partly in his reason.

THE PASSIONS THAT INCLINE MEN TO PEACE.

The passions that incline men to peace, are fear of death; desire of such things as are necessary to commodious living; and a hope by their industry to obtain them. And reason suggesteth convenient articles of peace, upon which men may be drawn to agreement. These articles, are they, which otherwise are called the Laws of Nature: whereof I shall speak more particularly, in the two following chapters.

CHAPTER XIV

OF THE FIRST AND SECOND NATURAL LAWS, AND OF CONTRACTS

RIGHT OF NATURE WHAT.

The right of nature, which writers commonly call *jus naturale*, is the liberty each man hath, to use his own power, as he will himself, for the preservation of his own nature; that is to say, of his own life; and consequently, of doing any thing, which in his own judgment, and reason, he shall conceive to be the aptest means thereunto.

LIBERTY WHAT.

By liberty, is understood, according to the proper signification of the word, the absence of external impediments: which impediments, may oft take away part of a man's power to do what he would; but cannot hinder him from using the power left him, according as his judgment, and reason shall dictate to him.

A LAW OF NATURE WHAT. DIFFERENCE OF RIGHT AND LAW.

A law of nature, *lex naturalis*, is a precept or general

rule, found out by reason, by which a man is forbidden to do that, which is destructive of his life, or taketh away the means of preserving the same; and to omit that, by which he thinketh it may be best preserved. For though they that speak of this subject, use to confound *jus*, and *lex*, right and law: yet they ought to be distinguished; because right, consisteth in liberty to do, or to forbear; whereas law, determineth, and bindeth to one of them: so that law, and right, differ as much, as obligation, and liberty; which in one and the same matter are inconsistent.

NATURALLY EVERY MAN HAS RIGHT TO EVERY THING.
THE FUNDAMENTAL LAW OF NATURE.

And because the condition of man, as hath been declared in the precedent chapter, is a condition of war of every one against every one; in which case every one is governed by his own reason; and there is nothing he can make use of, that may not be a help unto him, in preserving his life against his enemies; it followeth, that in such a condition, every man has a right to every thing; even to one another's body. And therefore, as long as this natural right of every man to every thing endureth, there can be no security to any man, how strong or wise soever he be, of living out the time, which nature ordinarily alloweth men to live. And consequently it is a precept, or general rule of reason, that every man, ought to endeavour peace, as far as he has hope of obtaining it; and when he cannot obtain it, that he may seek, and use, all helps, and advantages of war. The first branch of which rule, containeth the first, and fundamental law of nature; which is, *to seek peace, and follow it.* The second, the sum of the right of nature; which is, *by all means we can, to defend ourselves.*

THE SECOND LAW OF NATURE.

From this fundamental law of nature, by which men are commanded to endeavour peace, is derived this second law; *that a man be willing, when others are so too, as far-forth, as for peace, and defence of himself he shall think it necessary, to lay down this right to all things; and be contented with so much liberty against other men, as he would allow other men against himself.* For as long as every man holdeth this right, of doing any thing he liketh; so long are all men in the condition of war. But if other men will not lay down their right, as well as he; then there is no reason for any one, to divest himself of his: for that were to expose himself to prey, which no man is bound to, rather than to dispose himself to peace. This is that law of the Gospel; *whatsoever you require that others should do to you, that do ye to them.* And that law of all men, *quod tibi fieri non vis, alteri ne feceris.*

What it is to lay down a right.

To lay down a man's right to any thing, is to divest him-self of the liberty, of hindering another of the benefit of his own right to the same. For he that renounceth, or passeth away his right, giveth not to any other man a right which he had not before; because there is nothing to which every man had not right by nature: but only standeth out of his way, that he may enjoy his own orig-inal right, without hindrance from him; not without hindrance from another. So that the effect which redoundeth to one man, by another man's defect of right, is but so much diminution of impediments to the use of his own right original.

Renouncing a right, what it is. Transferring right what. Obligation. Duty. Injustice.

Right is laid aside, either by simply renouncing it; or by transferring it to another. By simply renouncing; when he cares not to whom the benefit thereof redoundeth. By transferring; when he intendeth the benefit thereof to some certain person, or persons. And when a man hath in either manner abandoned, or granted away his right; then is he said to be obliged, or bound, not to hinder those, to whom such right is granted, or aban-doned, from the benefit of it: and that he ought, and it is his duty, not to make void that voluntary act of his own: and that such hindrance is injustice, and injury, as being *sine jure*; the right being before renounced, or transferred. So that injury, or injustice, in the controversies of the world, is somewhat like to that, which in the disputations of scholars is called absurdity. For as it is there called an absurdity, to contradict what one maintained in the beginning: so in the world, it is called injustice, and injury, voluntarily to undo that, which from the beginning he had voluntarily done. The way by which a man either simply renounceth, or transferreth his right, is a declaration, or signification, by some voluntary and sufficient sign, or signs, that he doth so renounce, or transfer; or hath so renounced, or transferred the same, to him that accepteth it. And these signs are either words only, or actions only; or, as it happeneth most often, both words, and actions. And the same are the bonds, by which men are bound, and obliged: bonds, that have their strength, not from their own nature, for nothing is more easily broken than a man's word, but from fear of some evil consequence upon the rupture.

Not all rights are alienable.

Whensoever a man transferreth his right, or renounceth it; it is either in consideration of some right reciprocally transferred to himself; or for some other good he hopeth for thereby. For it is a voluntary act: and of the voluntary acts of every man, the object is some good to himself. And therefore there be some rights, which no man can be understood by any words, or other signs, to have abandoned, or transferred. As first a man cannot lay down the right of resisting them, that assault him by force, to take away his life; because he cannot be understood to aim thereby, at any good to himself. The same may be said of wounds, and chains, and imprisonment; both because there is no benefit consequent to such patience; as there is to the patience of suffering another to be wounded, or imprisoned: as also because a man cannot tell, when he seeth men proceed against him by violence, whether they intend his death or not. And lastly the motive, and end for which this renouncing, and transferring of right is introduced, is nothing else but the security of a man's person, in his life, and in the means of so preserving life, as not to be weary of it. And therefore if a man by words, or other signs, seem to despoil himself of the end, for which those signs were intended; he is not to be understood as if he meant it, or that it was his will; but that he was ignorant of how such words and actions were to be interpreted.

CONTRACT WHAT.

The mutual transferring of right, is that which men call contract.

There is difference between transferring of right to

the thing; and transferring, or tradition, that is delivery of the thing itself. For the thing may be delivered together with the translation of the right; as in buying and selling with ready-money; or exchange of goods, or lands: and it may be delivered some time after.

CONVENANT WHAT.

Again, one of the contractors, may deliver the thing contracted for on his part, and leave the other to perform his part at some determinate time after, and in the mean time be trusted; and then the contract on his part, is called pact, or covenant: or both parts may contract now, to perform hereafter: in which cases, he that is to perform in time to come, being trusted, his performance is called keeping of promise, or faith; and the failing of performance, if it be voluntary, violation of faith.

FREE-GIFT.

When the transferring of right, is not mutual: but one of the parties transferreth, in hope to gain thereby friendship, or service from another, or from his friends; or in hope to gain the reputation of charity, or magnanimity; or to deliver his mind from the pain of compassion; or in hope of reward in heaven; this is not contract, but gift, free-gift, grace: which words signify one and the same thing.

SIGNS OF CONTRACT EXPRESS. PROMISE.

Signs of contract, are either express, or by inference. Express, are words spoken with understanding of what they signify: and such words are either of the time present, or past; as, I give, I grant, I have given, I have granted, I will that this be yours: or of the future; as, I will give, I will grant: which words of the future are called promise.

SIGNS OF CONTRACT BY INFERENCE.

Signs by inference, are sometimes the consequence of words; sometimes the consequence of silence; sometimes the consequence of actions; sometimes the consequence of forbearing an action: and generally a sign by inference, of any contract, is whatsoever sufficiently argues the will of the contractor.

FREE GIFT PASSETH BY WORDS OF THE PRESENT OR PAST.

Words alone, if they be of the time to come, and contain a bare promise, are an insufficient sign of a free gift, and therefore not obligatory. For if they be of the time to come, as to-morrow I will give, they are a sign I have not given yet, and consequently that my right is not transferred, but remaineth till I transfer it by some other act. But if the words be of the time present, or past, as, I have given, or, do give to be delivered to-morrow, then is my to-morrow's right given away to day; and that by the virtue of the words, though there were no other argument of my will. And there is a great difference in the signification of these words, *volo hoc tuum esse cras*, and *cras dabo*; that is, between I will that this be thine to-morrow, and, I will give it thee to-morrow: for the word I will, in the former manner of speech, signifies an act of the will present; but in the latter, it signifies a promise of an act of the will to come: and therefore the former words, being of the present, transfer a future right; the latter, that be of the future, transfer nothing. But if there be other signs of the will to transfer a right, besides words; then, though the gift be free, yet may the right be understood to pass by words of the future: as if a man propound a prize to him that comes first to the end of a race, the gift is free; and though the words be of the future, yet the right passeth: for if he would not have his words so be understood, he should not have let them run.

SIGNS OF CONTRACT ARE WORDS BOTH OF THE PAST, PRESENT, AND FUTURE.

In contracts, the right passeth, not only where the words are of the time present, or past, but also where they are of the future: because all contract is mutual translation, or change of right; and therefore he that promiseth only, because he hath already received the benefit for which he promiseth, is to be understood as if he intended the right should pass: for unless he had

been content to have his words so understood, the
other would not have performed his part first. And for
that cause, in buying, and selling, and other acts of
contract, a promise is equivalent to a covenant; and
therefore obligatory.

MERIT WHAT.

He that performeth first in the case of a contract, is said
to merit that which he is to receive by the performance of
the other; and he hath it as due. Also when a prize is
propounded to many, which is to be given to him only
that winneth; or money is thrown amongst many, to be
enjoyed by them that catch it; though this be a free gift;
yet so to win, or so to catch, is to merit, and to have it as
due. For the right is transferred in the propounding of
the prize, and in throwing down the money; though it be
not determined to whom, but by the event of the contention. But there is between these two sorts of merit, this
difference, that in contract, I merit by virtue of my own
power, and the contractor's need; but in this case of free
gift, I am enabled to merit only by the benignity of the
giver: in contract, I merit at the contractor's hand that he
should depart with his right; in this case of gift, I merit
not that the giver should part with his right; but that
when he has parted with it, it should be mine, rather
than another's. And this I think to be the meaning of that
distinction of the Schools, between *meritum congrui*, and

meritum condigni. For God Almighty, having promised Paradise to those men, hoodwinked with carnal desires, that can walk through this world according to the precepts, and limits prescribed by him; they say, he that shall so walk, shall merit Paradise *ex congruo*. But because no man can demand a right to it, by his own righteousness, or any other power in himself, but by the free grace of God only; they say, no man can merit Paradise *ex condigno*. This I say, I think is the meaning of that distinction; but because disputers do not agree upon the signification of their own terms of art, longer than it serves their turn; I will not affirm any thing of their meaning: only this I say; when a gift is given indefinitely, as a prize to be contended for, he that winneth meriteth, and may claim the prize as due.

Covenants of mutual trust, when invalid.

If a covenant be made, wherein neither of the parties perform presently, but trust one another; in the condition of mere nature, which is a condition of war of every man against every man, upon any reasonable suspicion, it is void: but if there be a common power set over them both, with right and force sufficient to compel performance, it is not void. For he that performeth first, has no assurance the other will perform after; because the bonds of words are too weak to bridle men's ambition, avarice, anger, and other passions, without the fear of some coercive power; which in the condition of mere nature, where all men are equal, and judges of the justness of their own fears, cannot possibly be supposed. And therefore he which performeth first, does but betray himself to his enemy; contrary to the right, he can never abandon, of defending his life, and means of living.

But in a civil estate, where there is a power set up to constrain those that would otherwise violate their faith, that fear is no more reasonable; and for that cause, he which by the covenant is to perform first, is obliged so to do.

The cause of fear, which maketh such a covenant invalid, must be always something arising after the covenant made; as some new fact, or other sign of the will not to perform: else it cannot make the covenant void. For that which could not hinder a man from promising, ought not to be admitted as a hindrance of performing.

RIGHT TO THE END, CONTAINETH RIGHT TO THE MEANS.

He that transferreth any right, transferreth the means of enjoying it, as far as lieth in his power. As he that selleth land, is understood to transfer the herbage, and whatsoever grows upon it: nor can he that sells a mill turn away the stream that drives it. And they that give to a man the right of government in sovereignty, are understood to give him the right of levying money to maintain soldiers; and of appointing magistrates for the administration of justice.

No covenant with beasts.

To make covenants with brute beasts, is impossible; because not understanding our speech, they understand not, nor accept of any translation of right; nor can translate any right to another: and without mutual acceptation, there is no covenant.

Nor with God without special revelation.

To make covenant with God, is impossible, but by mediation of such as God speaketh to, either by revelation supernatural, or by his lieutenants that govern under him, and in his name: for otherwise we know not whether our covenants be accepted, or not. And therefore they that vow anything contrary to any law of nature, vow in vain; as being a thing unjust to pay such vow. And if it be a thing commanded by the law of nature, it is not the vow, but the law that binds them.

No covenant, but of possible and future.

The matter, or subject of a covenant, is always something that falleth under deliberation; for to covenant, is an act of the will; that is to say, an act, and the last act of deliberation; and is therefore always understood to be something to come; and which is judged possible for him that covenanteth, to perform.

And therefore, to promise that which is known to be impossible, is no covenant. But if that prove impossible afterwards, which before was thought possible, the covenant is valid, and bindeth, though not to the thing itself, yet to the value; or, if that also be impossible, to the unfeigned endeavour of performing as much as is possible: for to more no man can be obliged.

COVENANTS HOW MADE VOID.

Men are freed of their covenants two ways; by performing; or by being forgiven. For performance, is the natural end of obligation; and forgiveness, the restitution of liberty; as being a retransferring of that right, in which the obligation consisted.

COVENANTS EXTORTED BY FEAR ARE VALID.

Covenants entered into by fear, in the condition of mere nature, are obligatory. For example, if I covenant to pay a ransom, or service for my life, to an enemy; I am bound by it: for it is a contract, wherein one receiveth the benefit of life; the other is to receive money, or service for it; and consequently, where no other law, as in the condition of mere nature, forbiddeth the performance, the covenant is valid. Therefore prisoners of war, if trusted with the payment of their ransom, are obliged to pay it: and if a weaker prince, make a disadvantageous peace with a stronger, for fear; he is bound to keep it; unless, as hath been said before, there ariseth some new, and just cause of fear, to renew the war. And even in commonwealths, if I be forced to redeem myself from a thief by promising him money, I am bound to pay it, till the civil law discharge me. For whatsoever I may lawfully do without obligation, the same I may lawfully covenant to do through fear: and what I lawfully covenant, I cannot lawfully break.

THE FORMER COVENANT TO ONE, MAKES
VOID THE LATER TO ANOTHER.

A former covenant, makes void a later. For a man that hath passed away his right to one man to-day, hath it not to pass to-morrow to another: and therefore the later promise passeth no right, but is null.

A MAN'S COVENANT NOT TO DEFEND HIMSELF IS VOID.

A covenant not to defend myself from force, by force, is always void. For, as I have showed before, no man can transfer, or lay down his right to save himself from death, wounds, and imprisonment, the avoiding whereof is the only end of laying down any right; and therefore the promise of not resisting force, in no covenant transfer-reth any right; nor is obliging. For though a man may covenant thus, unless I do so, or so, kill me; he cannot covenant thus, unless I do so, or so, I will not resist you, when you come to kill me. For man by nature chooseth the lesser evil, which is danger of death in resisting; rather than the greater, which is certain and present death in not resisting. And this is granted to be true by all men, in that they lead criminals to execution, and prison, with armed men, notwithstanding that such criminals have consented to the law, by which they are condemned.

No man obliged to accuse himself.

A covenant to accuse oneself, without assurance of pardon, is likewise invalid. For in the condition of nature, where every man is judge, there is no place for accusation: and in the civil state, the accusation is followed with punishment; which being force, a man is not obliged not to resist. The same is also true, of the accusation of those, by whose condemnation a man falls into misery; as of a father, wife, or benefactor. For the testimony of such an accuser, if it be not willingly given, is presumed to be corrupted by nature; and therefore not to be received: and where a man's testimony is not to be credited, he is not bound to give it. Also accusations upon torture, are not to be reputed as testimonies. For torture is to be used but as means of conjecture, and light, in the further examination, and search of truth: and what is in that case confessed, tendeth to the ease of him that is tortured; not to the informing of the torturers: and therefore ought not to have the credit of a sufficient testimony: for whether he deliver himself by true, or false accusation, he does it by the right of preserving his own life.

THE END OF AN OATH. THE FORM OF AN OATH.

The force of words, being, as I have formerly noted, too weak to hold men to the performance of their covenants; there are in man's nature, but two imaginable helps to strengthen it. And those are either a fear of the consequence of breaking their word; or a glory, or pride in appearing not to need to break it. This latter is a generosity too rarely found to be presumed on, especially in the pursuers of wealth, command, or sensual pleasure; which are the greatest part of mankind. The passion to be reckoned upon, is fear; whereof there be two very general objects: one, the power of spirits invisible; the other, the power of those men they shall therein offend. Of these two, though the former be the greater power, yet the fear of the latter is commonly the greater fear. The fear of the former is in every man, his own religion: which hath place in the nature of man before civil society. The latter hath not so; at least not place enough, to keep men to their promises; because in the condition of mere nature, the inequality of power is not discerned, but by the event of battle. So that before the time of civil society, or in the interruption thereof by war, there is nothing can strengthen a covenant of peace agreed on, against the temptations of avarice, ambition, lust, or other strong desire, but the fear of that invisible power, which they every one worship as God; and fear as a revenger of their perfidy. All therefore that can be done between two men not subject to civil power, is to put one another to swear by the God he feareth: which swearing, or oath, is a form of speech, added to a promise; by which he that promiseth, signifieth, that unless he perform, he renounceth the mercy of his God, or calleth to him for vengeance on himself. Such was the heathen form, Let Jupiter kill me else, as I kill this beast. So is our form, I shall do thus, and thus, so help me God. And this, with the rites and ceremonies, which every one useth in his own religion, that the fear of breaking faith might be the greater.

No oath but by God.

By this it appears, that an oath taken according to any other form, or rite, than his, that sweareth, is in vain; and no oath: and that there is no swearing by any thing which the swearer thinks not God. For though men have sometimes used to swear by their kings, for fear, or flattery; yet they would have it thereby understood, they attributed to them divine honour. And that swearing unnecessarily by God, is but prophaning of his name: and swearing by other things, as men do in common discourse, is not swearing, but an impious custom, gotten by too much vehemence of talking.

AN OATH ADDS NOTHING TO THE OBLIGATION.

It appears also, that the oath adds nothing to the obligation. For a covenant, if lawful, binds in the sight of God, without the oath, as much as with it: if unlawful, bindeth not at all; though it be confirmed with an oath.

CHAPTER XV

OF OTHER LAWS OF NATURE

THE THIRD LAW OF NATURE, JUSTICE.

From that law of nature, by which we are obliged to transfer to another, such rights, as being retained, hinder the peace of mankind, there followeth a third; which is this, that men perform their covenants made: without which, covenants are in vain, and but empty words; and the right of all men to all things remaining, we are still in the condition of war.

JUSTICE AND INJUSTICE WHAT.

And in this law of nature, consisteth the fountain and original of justice. For where no covenant hath preceded, there hath no right been transferred, and every man has right to every thing; and consequently, no action can be unjust. But when a covenant is made, then to break it is unjust: and the definition of injustice, is no other than the not performance of covenant. And whatsoever is not unjust, is just.

JUSTICE AND PROPRIETY BEGIN WITH THE CONSTITUTION OF COMMONWEALTH.

But because covenants of mutual trust, where there is a fear of not performance on either part, as hath been said in the former chapter, are invalid; though the original of justice be the making of covenants; yet injustice actually there can be none, till the cause of such fear be taken away; which while men are in the natural condition of war, cannot be done. Therefore before the names of just, and unjust can have place, there must be some coercive power, to compel men equally to the performance of their covenants, by the terror of some punishment, greater than the benefit they expect by the breach of their covenant; and to make good that propriety, which by mutual contract men acquire, in recompense of the universal right they abandon: and such power there is none before the erection of a commonwealth. And this is also to be gathered out of the ordinary definition of justice in the Schools: for they say, that justice is the constant will of giving to every man his own. And therefore where there is no own, that is no propriety, there is no injustice; and where there is no coercive power erected, that is, where there is no commonwealth, there is no propriety; all men having right to all things: therefore where there is no commonwealth, there nothing is unjust. So that the nature of justice, consisteth in keeping of valid covenants: but the validity of covenants begins not but with the constitution of a civil power, sufficient to compel men to keep them: and then it is also that propriety begins.

JUSTICE NOT CONTRARY TO REASON.

The fool hath said in his heart, there is no such thing as justice; and sometimes also with his tongue; seriously alleging, that every man's conservation, and contentment, being committed to his own care, there could be no reason, why every man might not do what he thought conduced thereunto: and therefore also to make, or not make; keep, or not keep covenants, was not against reason, when it conduced to one's benefit. He does not therein deny, that there be covenants; and that they are sometimes broken, sometimes kept; and that such breach of them may be called injustice, and the observance of them justice: but he questioneth, whether injustice, taking away the fear of God, for the same fool hath said in his heart there is no God, may not sometimes stand with that reason, which dictateth to every man his own good; and particularly then, when it conduceth to such a benefit, as shall put a man in a condition, to neglect not only the dispraise, and revilings, but also the power of other men. The kingdom of God is gotten by violence: but what if it could be gotten by unjust violence? were it against reason so to get it, when it is impossible to receive hurt by it? and if it be not against reason, it is not against justice; or else justice is not to be approved for good. From such reasoning as this, successful wickedness hath obtained the name of virtue: and some that in all other things have disallowed the violation of faith; yet have allowed it, when it is for the getting of a kingdom. And the heathen that believed, that Saturn was deposed by his son Jupiter, believed nevertheless the same Jupiter to be the avenger of injustice: somewhat like to a piece of law in Coke's *Commentaries on Littleton*; where he says, if the right heir of the crown be attainted of treason; yet the crown shall descend to him, and eo instante the attainder be void: from which instances a man will be very prone to infer; that when the heir apparent of a kingdom, shall kill him that is in possession, though his father; you may call it injustice, or by what other name you will; yet it can never be against reason, seeing all the voluntary actions of men tend to the benefit of themselves; and those actions are most reasonable, that conduce most to their ends. This specious reasoning is nevertheless false.

For the question is not of promises mutual, where there is no security of performance on either side; as when there is no civil power erected over the parties promising; for such promises are no covenants: but either where one of the parties has performed already; or where there is a power to make him perform; there is the question whether it be against reason, that is, against the benefit of the other to perform, or not. And I say it is not against reason. For the manifestation whereof, we are to consider; first, that when a man doth a thing, which notwithstanding any thing can be foreseen, and reckoned on, tendeth to his own destruction, howsoever some accident which he could not expect, arriving may turn it to his benefit; yet such events do not make it reasonably or wisely done. Secondly, that in a condition of war, wherein every man to every man, for want of a common power to keep them all in awe, is an enemy, there is no man who can hope by his own strength, or wit, to defend himself from destruction, without the help of confederates; where every one expects the same defence by the confederation, that any one else does: and therefore he which declares he thinks it reason to deceive those that help him, can in reason expect no other means of safety, than what can be had from his own single power. He therefore that breaketh his covenant, and consequently declareth that he thinks he may with reason do so, cannot be received into any society, that unite themselves for peace and defence, but by the error of them that receive him; nor when he is received, be retained in it, without seeing the danger of their error; which errors a man cannot reasonably reckon upon as the means of his security: and therefore if he be left, or cast out of society, he perisheth; and if he live in society, it is by the errors of other men, which he could not foresee, nor reckon upon; and consequently against the reason of his preservation; and so, as all men that contribute not to his destruction, forbear him only out of ignorance of what is good for themselves.

As for the instance of gaining the secure and perpetual felicity of heaven, by any way; it is frivolous: there being but one way imaginable; and that is not breaking, but keeping of covenant.

And for the other instance of attaining sovereignty by rebellion; it is manifest, that though the event follow, yet because it cannot reasonably be expected, but rather the contrary; and because by gaining it so, others are taught to gain the same in like manner, the attempt thereof is against reason. Justice therefore, that is to say, keeping of covenant, is a rule of reason, by which we are forbidden to do any thing destructive to our life; and consequently a law of nature.

There be some that proceed further; and will not have the law of nature, to be those rules which conduce to the preservation of man's life on earth; but to the attaining of an eternal felicity after death; to which they think the breach of covenant may conduce; and consequently be just and reasonable; such are they that think it a work of merit to kill, or depose, or rebel against, the sovereign power constituted over them by their own consent. But because there is no natural knowledge of man's estate after death; much less of the reward that is then to be given to breach of faith; but only a belief grounded upon other men's saying, that they know it supernaturally, or that they know those, that knew them, that knew others, that knew it super-naturally; breach of faith cannot be called a precept of reason, or nature.

COVENANTS NOT DISCHARGED BY THE VICE OF THE PERSON TO WHOM THEY ARE MADE.

Others, that allow for a law of nature, the keeping of faith, do nevertheless make exception of certain persons; as heretics, and such as use not to perform their covenant to others: and this also is against reason. For if any fault of a man, be sufficient to discharge our covenant made; the same ought in reason to have been sufficient to have hindered the making of it.

JUSTICE OF MEN AND JUSTICE OF ACTIONS WHAT.

The names of just, and injust, when they are attributed to men, signify one thing; and when they are attributed to actions, another. When they are attributed to men, they signify conformity, or inconformity of manners, to reason. But when they are attributed to actions, they signify the conformity, or inconformity to reason, not of manners, or manner of life, but of particular actions. A just man therefore, is he that taketh all the care he can, that his actions may be all just: and an unjust man, is he that neglecteth it. And such men are more often in our language styled by the names of righteous, and unrighteous; than just, and unjust; though the meaning be the same. Therefore a righteous man, does not lose that title, by one, or a few unjust actions, that proceed from sudden passion, or mistake of things, or persons: nor does an unrighteous man, lose his character, for such actions, as he does, or forbears to do, for fear: because his will is not framed by the justice, but by the apparent benefit of what he is to do. That which gives to human actions the relish of justice, is a certain nobleness or gallantness of courage, rarely found, by which a man scorns to be beholden for the contentment of his life, to fraud, or breach of promise. This justice of the manners, is that which is meant, where justice is called a virtue; and injustice a vice.

But the justice of actions donominates men, not just, but guiltless: and the injustice of the same, which is also called injury, gives them but the name of guilty.

JUSTICE OF MANNERS, AND JUSTICE OF ACTIONS.

Again, the injustice of manners, is the disposition, or aptitude to do injury; and is injustice before it proceed to act; and without supposing any individual person injured. But the injustice of an action, that is to say injury, supposeth an individual person injured; namely him, to whom the covenant was made: and therefore many times the injury is received by one man, when the damage redoundeth to another. As when the master commandeth his servant to give money to a stranger; if it be not done, the injury is done to the master, whom he had before covenanted to obey; but the damage redoundeth to the stranger, to whom he had no obligation; and therefore could not injure him. And so also in commonwealths, private men may remit to one another their debts; but not robberies or other violences, whereby they are endamaged; because the detaining of debt, is an injury to themselves; but robbery and violence, are injuries to the person of the commonwealth.

NOTHING DONE TO A MAN BY HIS
OWN CONSENT CAN BE INJURY.

Whatsoever is done to a man, conformable to his own will signified to the doer, is no injury to him. For if he that doeth it, hath not passed away his original right to do what he please, by some antecedent covenant, there is no breach of covenant; and therefore no injury done

him. And if he have; then his will to have it done being
signified, is a release of that covenant: and so again there
is no injury done him.

JUSTICE COMMUTATIVE AND DISTRIBUTIVE.

Justice of actions, is by writers divided into commutative, and distributive: and the former they say consisteth
in proportion arithmetical; the latter in proportion geo-
metrical. Commutative therefore, they place in the
equality of value of the things contracted for; and distributive, in the distribution of equal benefit, to men of
equal merit. As if it were injustice to sell dearer than we
buy; or to give more to a man than he merits. The value
of all things contracted for, is measured by the appetite
of the contractors: and therefore the just value, is that
which they be contented to give. And merit, besides that
which is by covenant, where the performance on one
part, meriteth the performance of the other part, and
falls under justice commutative, not distributive, is not
due by justice; but is rewarded of grace only. And therefore this distinction, in the sense wherein it useth to be
expounded, is not right. To speak properly, commutative justice, is the justice, of a contractor; that is, a performance of covenant, in buying, and selling; hiring,
and letting to hire; lending, and borrowing; exchanging,
bartering, and other acts of contract.

And distributive justice, the justice of an arbitrator;

that is to say, the act of defining what is just. Wherein, being trusted by them that make him arbitrator, if he perform his trust, he is said to distribute to every man his own: and this is indeed just distribution, and may be called, though improperly, distributive justice; but more properly equity; which also is a law of nature, as shall be shown in due place.

THE FOURTH LAW OF NATURE, GRATITUDE.

As justice dependeth on antecedent covenant; so does gratitude depend on antecedent grace; that is to say, antecedent free gift: and is the fourth law of nature; which may be conceived in this form, that a man which receiveth benefit from another of mere grace, endeavour that he which giveth it, have no reasonable cause to repent him of his good will. For no man giveth, but with intention of good to himself; because gift is voluntary; and of all voluntary acts, the object is to every man his own good; of which if men see they shall be frustrated, there will be no beginning of benevolence, or trust; nor consequently of mutual help; nor of reconciliation of one man to another; and therefore they are to remain still in the condition of war; which is contrary to the first and fundamental law of nature, which commandeth men to seek peace. The breach of this law, is called ingratitude; and hath the same relation to grace, that injustice hath to obligation by covenant.

THE FIFTH MUTUAL ACCOMMODATION, OR COMPLAISANCE.

A fifth law of nature, is complaisance; that is to say, that every man strive to accommodate himself to the rest. For the understanding whereof, we may consider, that there is in men's aptness to society, a diversity of nature, rising from their diversity of affections; not unlike to that we see in stones brought together for building of an edifice. For as that stone which by the asperity, and irregularity of figure, takes more room from others, than itself fills; and for the hardness, cannot be easily made plain, and thereby hindereth the building, is by the builders cast away as unprofitable, and troublesome: so also, a man that by asperity of nature, will strive to retain those things which to himself are superfluous, and to others necessary; and for the stubbornness of his passions, cannot be corrected, is to be left, or cast out of society, as cumbersome thereunto. For seeing every man, not only by right, but also by necessity of nature, is supposed to endeavour all he can, to obtain that which is necessary for his conservation; he that shall oppose himself against it, for things superfluous, is guilty of the war that thereupon is to follow; and therefore doth that, which is contrary to the fundamental law of nature, which commandeth to seek peace. The observers of this law, may be called sociable, the Latins call them commodi; the contrary, stubborn, insociable, froward, intractable.

THE SIXTH, FACILITY TO PARDON.

A sixth law of nature, is this, that upon caution of the future time, a man ought to pardon the offences past of them that repenting, desire it. For pardon, is nothing but granting of peace; which though granted to them that persevere in their hostility, be not peace, but fear; yet not granted to them that give caution of the future time, is sign of an aversion to peace; and therefore contrary to the law of nature.

THE SEVENTH, THAT IN REVENGES, MEN
RESPECT ONLY THE FUTURE GOOD.

A seventh is, that in revenges, that is, retribution of evil for evil, men look not at the greatness of the evil past, but the greatness of the good to follow. Whereby we are forbidden to inflict punishment with any other design, than for correction of the offender, or direction of others. For this law is consequent to the next before it, that commandeth pardon, upon security of the future time. Besides, revenge without respect to the example, and profit to come, is a triumph, or glorying in the hurt of another, tending to no end; for the end is always somewhat to come; and glorying to no end, is vain-glory, and contrary to reason, and to hurt without reason, tendeth to the introduction of war; which is against the law of nature; and is commonly styled by the name of cruelty.

The eighth, against contumely.

And because all signs of hatred, or contempt, provoke
to fight; insomuch as most men choose rather to hazard
their life, than not to be revenged; we may in the eighth
place, for a law of nature, set down this precept, that no
man by deed, word, countenance, or gesture, declare
hatred, or contempt of another. The breach of which
law, is commonly called contumely.

The ninth, against pride.

The question who is the better man, has no place in the
condition of mere nature; where, as has been shewn before,
all men are equal. The inequality that now is, has been
introduced by the laws civil. I know that Aristotle in the
first book of his Politics, for a foundation of his doctrine,
maketh men by nature, some more worthy to command,
meaning the wiser sort, such as he thought himself to be
for his philosophy; others to serve, meaning those that
had strong bodies, but were not philosophers as he; as if
master and servant were not introduced by consent of
men, but by difference of wit: which is not only against
reason; but also against experience. For there are very few
so foolish, that had not rather govern themselves, than be
governed by others: nor when the wise in their own conceit, contend by force, with them who distrust their own
wisdom, do they always, or often, or almost at any time,
get the victory. If nature therefore have made men equal,

that equality is to be acknowledged: or if nature have made men unequal; yet because men that think themselves equal, will not enter into conditions of peace, but upon equal terms, such equality must be admitted. And therefore for the ninth law of nature, I put this, that every man acknowledge another for his equal by nature. The breach of this precept is pride.

THE TENTH, AGAINST ARROGANCE.

On this law, dependeth another, that at the entrance into conditions of peace, no man require to reserve to himself any right, which he is not content should be reserved to every one of the rest. As it is necessary for all men that seek peace, to lay down certain rights of nature; that is to say, not to have liberty to do all they list: so is it necessary for man's life, to retain some; as right to govern their own bodies; enjoy air, water, motion, ways to go from place to place; and all things else, without which a man cannot live, or not live well. If in this case, at the making of peace, men require for themselves, that which they would not have to be granted to others, they do contrary to the precedent law, that commandeth the acknowledgment of natural equality, and therefore also against the law of nature. The observers of this law, are those we call modest, and the breakers arrogant men. The Greeks call the violation of this law πλεονεξια; that is, a desire of more than their share.

The eleventh, equity.

Also if a man be trusted to judge between man and man, it is a precept of the law of nature, that he deal equally between them. For without that, the controversies of men cannot be determined but by war. He therefore that is partial in judgment, doth what in him lies, to deter men from the use of judges, and arbitrators; and consequently, against the fundamental law of nature, is the cause of war.

The observance of this law, from the equal distribution to each man, of that which in reason belongeth to him, is called equity, and, as I have said before, distributive justice: the violation, acception of persons, προσωποληψία.

The twelfth, equal use of things common.

And from this followeth another law, that such things as cannot be divided, be enjoyed in common, if it can be; and if the quantity of the thing permit, without stint; otherwise proportionably to the number of them that have right. For otherwise the distribution is unequal, and contrary to equity.

The thirteenth, of lot.

But some things there be, that can neither be divided, nor enjoyed in common. Then, the law of nature, which prescribeth equity, requireth, that the entire right; or else, making the use alternate, the first possession, be determined by lot. For equal distribution, is of the law of nature; and other means of equal distribution cannot be imagined.

THE FOURTEENTH, OF PRIMOGENITURE, AND FIRST SEIZING.

Of lots there be two sorts, arbitrary, and natural. Arbitrary, is that which is agreed on by the competitors: natural, is either primogeniture, which the Greek calls κληρονομία, which signifies, given by lot; or first seizure.

And therefore those things which cannot be enjoyed in common, nor divided, ought to be adjudged to the first possessor; and in some cases to the first born, as acquired by lot.

THE FIFTEENTH, OF MEDIATORS.

It is also a law of nature, that all men that mediate peace, be allowed safe conduct. For the law that commandeth peace, as the end, commandeth intercession, as the means; and to intercession the means is safe conduct.

THE SIXTEENTH, OF SUBMISSION TO ARBITREMENT.

And because, though men be never so willing to observe these laws, there may nevertheless arise questions concerning a man's action; first, whether it were done, or not done; secondly, if done, whether against the law, or

not against the law; the former whereof, is called a question of fact; the latter a question of right, therefore
unless the parties to the question, covenant mutually to
stand to the sentence of another, they are as far from
peace as ever. This other to whose sentence they submit
is called an arbitrator. And therefore it is of the law of
nature, that they that are at controversy, submit their
right to the judgment of an arbitrator.

The seventeenth, no man is his own judge.

And seeing every man is presumed to do all things in
order to his own benefit, no man is a fit arbitrator in his
own cause; and if he were never so fit; yet equity allowing to each party equal benefit, if one be admitted to be
judge, the other is to be admitted also; and so the controversy, that is, the cause of war, remains, against the
law of nature.

The eighteenth, no man to be judge, that
has in him a natural cause of partiality.

For the same reason no man in any cause ought to be
received for arbitrator, to whom greater profit, or honour, or pleasure apparently ariseth out of the victory of
one party, than of the other: for he hath taken, though an
unavoidable bribe, yet a bribe; and no man can be obliged
to trust him. And thus also the controversy, and the condition of war remaineth, contrary to the law of nature.

The nineteenth, of witnesses.

And in a controversy of fact, the judge being to give no more credit to one, than to the other, if there be no other arguments, must give credit to a third; or to a third and fourth; or more: for else the question is undecided, and left to force, contrary to the law of nature.

These are the laws of nature, dictating peace, for a means of the conservation of men in multitudes; and which only concern the doctrine of civil society. There be other things tending to the destruction of particular men; as drunkenness, and all other parts of intemperance; which may therefore also be reckoned amongst those things which the law of nature hath forbidden; but are not necessary to be mentioned, nor are pertinent enough to this place.

A rule, by which the laws of nature
may easily be examined.

And though this may seem too subtle a deduction of the laws of nature, to be taken notice of by all men; whereof the most part are too busy in getting food, and the rest too negligent to understand; yet to leave all men inexcusable, they have been contracted into one easy sum, intelligible even to the meanest capacity; and that is, Do not that to another, which thou wouldest not have done to thyself; which sheweth him, that he has no more to do in learning the laws of nature, but, when weighing the actions of other men with his own, they seem too heavy, to put them into the other part of the balance, and his own into their place, that his own passions, and self-love, may add nothing to the weight; and then there is none of these laws of nature that will not appear unto him very reasonable.

THE LAWS OF NATURE OBLIGE IN CONSCIENCE ALWAYS, BUT IN EFFECT THEN ONLY WHEN THERE IS SECURITY.

The laws of nature oblige *in foro interno*; that is to say, they bind to a desire they should take place: but *in foro externo*; that is, to the putting them in act, not always. For he that should be modest, and tractable, and perform all he promises, in such time, and place, where no man else should do so, should but make himself a prey to others, and procure his own certain ruin, contrary to the ground of all laws of nature, which tend to nature's preservation. And again, he that having sufficient security, that others shall observe the same laws towards him, observes them not himself, seeketh not peace, but war; and consequently the destruction of his nature by violence.

And whatsoever laws bind *in foro interno*, may be broken, not only by a fact contrary to the law, but also by a fact according to it, in case a man think it contrary. For though his action in this case, be according to the law; yet his purpose was against the law; which, where the obligation is *in foro interno*, is a breach.

THE LAWS OF NATURE ARE ETERNAL.

The laws of nature are immutable and eternal; for injustice, ingratitude, arrogance, pride, iniquity, acception of persons, and the rest, can never be made lawful. For it can never be that war shall preserve life, and peace destroy it.

AND YET EASY.

The same laws, because they oblige only to a desire, and endeavour, I mean an unfeigned and constant endeavour, are easy to be observed. For in that they require nothing but endeavour, he that endeavoureth their performance, fulfilleth them; and he that fulfilleth the law, is just.

THE SCIENCE OF THESE LAWS, IS THE
TRUE MORAL PHILOSOPHY.

And the science of them, is the true and only moral philosophy. For moral philosophy is nothing else but the science of what is good, and evil, in the conversation, and society of mankind. Good, and evil, are names that signify our appetites, and aversions; which in different tempers, customs, and doctrines of men, are different; and divers men, differ not only in their judgment, on the senses of what is pleasant, and unpleasant to the taste, smell, hearing, touch, and sight; but also of what is conformable, or disagreeable to reason, in the actions of common life. Nay, the same man, in divers times, differs from himself; and one time praiseth, that is, calleth good, what another time he dispraiseth, and calleth evil: from whence arise disputes, controversies, and at last war. And therefore so long as a man is in the condition of mere nature, which is a condition of war, as private appetite is the measure of good, and evil: and consequently all men agree on this, that peace is good, and therefore also the way, or means of peace, which, as I have shewed before, are justice, gratitude, modesty, equity, mercy, and the rest of the laws of nature, are good; that is to say; moral virtues; and their contrary vices, evil. Now the science of virtue and vice, is moral philosophy; and therefore the true doctrine of the laws of nature, is the true moral philosophy. But the writers of moral philosophy, though they acknowledge the same virtues and vices; yet not seeing wherein consisted their goodness; nor that they come to be praised, as the means of peaceable, sociable, and comfortable living, place them in a mediocrity of passions: as if not the cause, but the degree of daring, made fortitude; or not the cause, but the quantity of a gift, made liberality.

These dictates of reason, men used to call by the name of laws, but improperly: for they are but conclusions, or theorems concerning what conduceth to the conservation and defence of themselves; whereas law, properly, is the word of him, that by right hath command over others. But yet if we consider the same theorems, as delivered in the word of God, that by right commandeth all things; then are they properly called laws.

CHAPTER XVII

OF THE CAUSES, GENERATION, AND DEFINITION OF A

COMMONWEALTH

THE END OF COMMONWEALTH, PARTICULAR SECURITY.
The final cause, end, or design of men, who naturally love liberty, and dominion over others, in the introduction of that restraint upon themselves, in which we see them live in commonwealths, is the foresight of their own preservation, and of a more contented life thereby; that is to say, of getting themselves out from that miserable condition of war, which is necessarily consequent, as hath been shown in chapter XIII, to the natural passions of men, when there is no visible power to keep them in awe, and tie them by fear of punishment to the performance of their covenants, and observation of those laws of nature set down in the fourteenth and fifteenth chapters.

WHICH IS NOT TO BE HAD FROM THE LAW OF NATURE.
For the laws of nature, as justice, equity, modesty, mercy, and, in sum, doing to others, as we would be done to, of themselves, without the terror of some power, to cause them to be observed, are contrary to our natural pas-

sions, that carry us to partiality, pride, revenge, and the like. And covenants, without the sword, are but words, and of no strength to secure a man at all. Therefore notwithstanding the laws of nature, which every one hath then kept, when he has the will to keep them, when he can do it safely, if there be no power erected, or not great enough for our security; every man will, and may lawfully rely on his own strength and art, for caution against all other men. And in all places, where men have lived by small families, to rob and spoil one another, has been a trade, and so far from being reputed against the law of nature, that the greater spoils they gained, the greater was their honour; and men observed no other laws therein, but the laws of honour; that is, to abstain from cruelty, leaving to men their lives, and instruments of husbandry. And as small families did then; so now do cities and kingdoms which are but greater families, for their own security, enlarge their dominions, upon all pretences of danger, and fear of invasion, or assistance that may be given to invaders, and endeavour as much as they can, to subdue, or weaken their neighbours, by open force, and secret arts, for want of other caution, justly; and are remembered for it in after ages with honour.

NOR FROM THE CONJUNCTION OF A FEW MEN OR FAMILIES.
Nor is it the joining together of a small number of men, that gives them this security; because in small numbers,

small additions on the one side or the other, make the advantage of strength so great, as is sufficient to carry the victory; and therefore gives encouragement to an invasion. The multitude sufficient to confide in for our security, is not determined by any certain number, but by comparison with the enemy we fear; and is then sufficient, when the odds of the enemy is not of so visible and conspicuous moment, to determine the event of war, as to move him to attempt.

Nor from a great multitude, unless directed by one judgment.

And be there never so great a multitude; yet if their actions be directed according to their particular judgments, and particular appetites, they can expect thereby no defence, nor protection, neither against a common enemy, nor against the injuries of one another. For being distracted in opinions concerning the best use and application of their strength, they do not help but hinder one another; and reduce their strength by mutual opposition to nothing: whereby they are easily, not only subdued by a very few that agree together; but also when there is no common enemy, they make war upon each other, for their particular interests. For if we could suppose a great multitude of men to consent in the observation of justice, and other laws of nature, without a common power to keep them all in awe; we might as

well suppose all mankind to do the same; and then
there neither would be, nor need to be any civil government, or commonwealth at all; because there would be
peace without subjection.

AND THAT CONTINUALLY.

Nor is it enough for the security, which men desire
should last all the time of their life, that they be governed, and directed by one judgment, for a limited time;
as in one battle, or one war. For though they obtain a
victory by their unanimous endeavour against a foreign
enemy; yet afterwards, when either they have no common enemy, or he that by one part is held for an enemy,
is by another part held for a friend, they must needs by
the difference of their interests dissolve, and fall again
into a war amongst themselves.

WHY CERTAIN CREATURES WITHOUT REASON, OR SPEECH, DO NEVERTHELESS LIVE IN SOCIETY, WITHOUT ANY COERCIVE POWER.

It is true, that certain living creatures, as bees, and ants,
live sociably one with another, which are therefore by
Aristotle numbered amongst political creatures; and yet
have no other direction, than their particular judgments
and appetites; nor speech, whereby one of them can signify to another, what he thinks expedient for the common benefit: and therefore some man may perhaps

desire to know, why mankind cannot do the same. To
which I answer,

First, that men are continually in competition for
honour and dignity, which these creatures are not; and
consequently amongst men there ariseth on that
ground, envy and hatred, and finally war; but amongst
these not so.

Secondly, that amongst these creatures, the common good differeth not from the private; and being by
nature inclined to their private, they procure thereby
the common benefit. But man, whose joy consisteth in
comparing himself with other men, can relish nothing
but what is eminent.

Thirdly, that these creatures, having not, as man,
the use of reason, do not see, nor think they see any
fault, in the administration of their common business;
whereas amongst men, there are very many, that think
themselves wiser, and abler to govern the public, better
than the rest; and these strive to reform and innovate,
one this way, another that way; and thereby bring it into
distraction and civil war.

Fourthly, that these creatures, though they have
some use of voice, in making known to one another
their desires, and other affections; yet they want that art
of words, by which some men can represent to others,
that which is good, in the likeness of evil; and evil, in
the likeness of good; and augment, or diminish the

apparent greatness of good and evil; discontenting men, and troubling their peace at their pleasure.

Fifthly, irrational creatures cannot distinguish between injury, and damage; and therefore as long as they be at ease, they are not offended with their fellows: whereas man is then most troublesome, when he is most at ease: for then it is that he loves to shew his wisdom, and control the actions of them that govern the commonwealth.

Lastly, the agreement of these creatures is natural; that of men, is by covenant only, which is artificial: and therefore it is no wonder if there be somewhat else required, besides covenant, to make their agreement constant and lasting; which is a common power, to keep them in awe, and to direct their actions to the common benefit.

THE GENERATION OF A COMMONWEALTH.
THE DEFINITION OF A COMMONWEALTH.

The only way to erect such a common power, as may be able to defend them from the invasion of foreigners, and the injuries of one another, and thereby to secure them in such sort, as that by their own industry, and by the fruits of the earth, they may nourish themselves and live contentedly; is, to confer all their power and strength upon one man, or upon one assembly of men, that may reduce all their wills, by plurality of voices, unto one

will: which is as much as to say, to appoint one man, or
assembly of men, to bear their person; and every one to
own, and acknowledge himself to be author of whatsoever he that so beareth their person, shall act, or cause to
be acted, in those things which concern the common
peace and safety; and therein to submit their wills, every
one to his will, and their judgments, to his judgment.
This is more than consent, or concord; it is a real unity
of them all, in one and the same person, made by covenant of every man with every man, in such manner, as if
every man should say to every man, I authorise and give
up my right of governing myself, to this man, or to this
assembly of men, on this condition, that thou give up
thy right to him, and authorize all his actions in like
manner. This done, the multitude so united in one person, is called a commonwealth, in Latin civitas. This is
the generation of that great leviathan, or rather, to speak
more reverently, of that mortal god, to which we owe
under the immortal God, our peace and defence. For by
this authority, given him by every particular man in the
commonwealth, he hath the use of so much power and
strength conferred on him, that by terror thereof, he is
enabled to perform the wills of them all, to peace at
home, and mutual aid against their enemies abroad. And
in him consisteth the essence of the commonwealth;
which, to define it, is one person, of whose acts a great
multitude, by mutual covenants one with another, have

made themselves every one the author, to the end he may use the strength and means of them all, as he shall think expedient, for their peace and common defence.

SOVEREIGN, AND SUBJECT, WHAT.

And he that carrieth this person, is called sovereign, and said to have sovereign power; and every one besides, his subject.

The attaining to this sovereign power, is by two ways. One, by natural force; as when a man maketh his children, to submit themselves, and their children to his government, as being able to destroy them if they refuse; or by war subdueth his enemies to his will, giving them their lives on that condition. The other, is when men agree amongst themselves, to submit to some man, or assembly of men, voluntarily, on confidence to be protected by him against all others. This latter, may be called a political commonwealth, or commonwealth by institution; and the former, a commonwealth by acquisition. And first, I shall speak of a commonwealth by institution.

CHAPTER XVIII

OF THE RIGHTS OF SOVEREIGNS BY INSTITUTION

THE ACT OF INSTITUTING A COMMONWEALTH, WHAT.

A commonwealth is said to be instituted, when a multitude of men do agree, and covenant, every one, with every one, that to whatsoever man, or assembly of men, shall be given by the major part, the right to present the person of them all, that is to say, to be their representative; every one, as well he that voted for it, as he that voted against it, shall authorize all the actions and judgments, of that man, or assembly of men, in the same manner, as if they were his own, to the end, to live peaceably amongst themselves, and be protected against other men.

THE CONSEQUENCES TO SUCH INSTITUTION, ARE.

From this institution of a commonwealth are derived all the rights, and faculties of him, or them, on whom sovereign power is conferred by the consent of the people assembled.

THE SUBJECTS CANNOT CHANGE THE FORM OF GOVERNMENT.

First, because they covenant, it is to be understood, they are not obliged by former covenant to anything repugnant hereunto. And consequently they that have already instituted a commonwealth, being thereby bound by covenant, to own the actions, and judgments of one, cannot lawfully make a new covenant, amongst themselves, to be obedient to any other, in any thing whatsoever, without his permission. And therefore, they that are subjects to a monarch, cannot without his leave cast off monarchy, and return to the confusion of a disunited multitude; nor transfer their person from him that beareth it, to another man, or other assembly of men: for they are bound, every man to every man, to own, and be reputed author of all, that he that already is their sovereign, shall do, and judge fit to be done: so that any one man dissenting, all the rest should break their covenant made to that man, which is injustice: and they have also every man given the sovereignty to him that beareth their person; and therefore if they depose him, they take from him that which is his own, and so again it is injustice. Besides, if he that attempteth to depose his sovereign, be killed, or punished by him for such attempt, he is author of his own punishment, as being by the institution, author of all his sovereign shall do: and because it is injustice for a man to do anything, for which he may be punished by his own authority, he is also upon that title, unjust. And whereas some men have pretended for their disobedience to their sovereign, a new covenant, made, not with men, but with God; this also is unjust: for there is no covenant with God, but by mediation of somebody that representeth God's person; which none doth but God's lieutenant, who hath the sovereignty under God. But this pretence of covenant with God, is so evident a lie, even in the pretenders' own consciences, that it is not only an act of an unjust, but also of a vile, and unmanly disposition.

SOVEREIGN POWER CANNOT BE FORFEITED.

Secondly, because the right of bearing the person of them all, is given to him they make sovereign, by covenant only of one to another, and not of him to any of them; there can happen no breach of covenant on the part of the sovereign; and consequently none of his subjects, by any pretence of forfeiture, can be freed from his subjection. That he which is made sovereign maketh no covenant with his subjects beforehand, is manifest; because either he must make it with the whole multitude, as one party to the covenant; or he must make a several covenant with every man. With the whole, as one party, it is impossible; because as yet they are not one person: and if he make so many several covenants as there be men, those covenants after he hath the sovereignty are void; because what act soever can be pretended by any one of them for breach thereof is the act both of himself, and of all the rest, because done in the person, and by the right of every one of them in particular. Besides, if any one, or more of them, pretend a breach of the covenant made by the sovereign at his institution; and others, or one other of his subjects, or himself alone, pretend there was no such breach, there is in this case, no judge to decide the controversy; it returns therefore to the sword again; and every man recovereth the right of protecting himself by his own strength, contrary to the design they had in the institution. It is therefore in vain to grant sovereignty by way of precedent covenant. The opinion that any monarch receiveth his power by covenant, that is to say, on condition, proceedeth from want of understanding this easy truth, that covenants being but words and breath, have no force to oblige, contain, constrain, or protect any man, but what it has from the public sword; that is, from the untied hands of that man, or assembly of men that hath the sovereignty, and whose actions are avouched by them all, and performed by the strength of them all, in him united. But when an assembly of men is made sovereign; then no man imagineth any such covenant to have passed in the institution; for no man is so dull as to say, for example, the people of Rome made a covenant with the Romans, to hold the sovereignty on such or such conditions; which not performed, the Romans might lawfully depose the Roman people. That men see not the reason to be alike in a monarchy, and in a popular government, proceedeth from the ambition of some, that are kinder to the government of an assembly, whereof they may hope to participate, than of monarchy, which they despair to enjoy.

No man can without injustice protest against the institution of the sovereign declared by the major part.

Thirdly, because the major part hath by consenting voices declared a sovereign; he that dissented must now consent with the rest; that is, be contented to avow all the actions he shall do, or else justly be destroyed by the rest. For if he voluntarily entered into the congregation of them that were assembled, he sufficiently declared thereby his will, and therefore tacitly covenanted, to stand to what the major part should ordain: and therefore if he refuse to stand thereto, or make protestation against any of their decrees, he does contrary to his covenant, and therefore unjustly. And whether he be of the congregation, or not; and whether his consent be asked, or not, he must either submit to their decrees, or be left in the condition of war he was in before; wherein he might without injustice be destroyed by any man whatsoever.

THE SOVEREIGN'S ACTIONS CANNOT BE
JUSTLY ACCUSED BY THE SUBJECT.

Fourthly, because every subject is by this institution author of all the actions, and judgments of the sovereign instituted; it follows, that whatsoever he doth, it can be no injury to any of his subjects; nor ought he to be by any of them accused of injustice. For he that doth anything by authority from another, doth therein no injury to him by whose authority he acteth: but by this institution of a commonwealth, every particular man is author of all the sovereign doth: and consequently he that complaineth of injury from his sovereign, com-

plaineth of that whereof he himself is author; and therefore ought not to accuse any man but himself; no nor
himself of injury; because to do injury to one's self, is
impossible. It is true that they that have sovereign power
may commit iniquity; but not injustice, or injury in the
proper signification.

WHATSOEVER THE SOVEREIGN DOTH IS UNPUNISHABLE BY THE SUBJECT.

Fifthly, and consequently to that which was said last, no
man that hath sovereign power can justly be put to
death, or otherwise in any manner by his subjects punished. For seeing every subject is author of the actions
of his sovereign; he punisheth another for the actions
committed by himself.

THE SOVEREIGN IS JUDGE OF WHAT IS NECESSARY FOR THE PEACE AND DEFENCE OF HIS SUBJECTS.

And because the end of this institution, is the peace and
defence of them all; and whosoever has right to the end,
has right to the means; it belongeth of right, to whatsoever man, or assembly that hath the sovereignty, to be
judge both of the means of peace and defence, and also
of the hindrances, and disturbances of the same; and to
do whatsoever he shall think necessary to be done, both
beforehand, for the preserving of peace and security, by
prevention of discord at home, and hostility from

abroad; and, when peace and security are lost, for the
recovery of the same. And therefore,

AND JUDGE OF WHAT DOCTRINES
ARE FIT TO BE TAUGHT THEM.

Sixthly, it is annexed to the sovereignty, to be judge of
what opinions and doctrines are averse, and what conducing to peace; and consequently, on what occasions,
how far, and what men are to be trusted withal, in
speaking to multitudes of people; and who shall examine the doctrines of all books before they be published.
For the actions of men proceed from their opinions;
and in the well-governing of opinions, consisteth the
well-governing of men's actions, in order to their peace,
and concord. And though in matter of doctrine, nothing ought to be regarded but the truth; yet this is not
repugnant to regulating the same by peace. For doctrine
repugnant to peace, can no more be true, than peace
and concord can be against the law of nature. It is true,
that in a commonwealth, where by the negligence, or
unskilfulness of governors, and teachers, false doctrines
are by time generally received; the contrary truths may
be generally offensive. Yet the most sudden, and rough
bursting in of a new truth, that can be, does never break
the peace, but only sometimes awake the war. For those
men that are so remissly governed, that they dare take
up arms to defend, or introduce an opinion, are still in

war; and their condition not peace, but only a cessation of arms for fear of one another; and they live, as it were, in the precincts of battle continually. It belongeth therefore to him that hath the sovereign power, to be judge, or constitute all judges of opinions and doctrines, as a thing necessary to peace; thereby to prevent discord and civil war.

THE RIGHT OF MAKING RULES; WHEREBY THE SUBJECTS MAY EVERY MAN KNOW WHAT IS SO HIS OWN, AS NO OTHER SUBJECT CAN WITHOUT INJUSTICE TAKE IT FROM HIM.

Seventhly, is annexed to the sovereignty, the whole power of prescribing the rules, whereby every man may know, what goods he may enjoy, and what actions he may do, without being molested by any of his fellow-subjects; and this is it men call propriety. For before constitution of sovereign power, as hath already been shown, all men had right to all things; which necessarily causeth war: and therefore this propriety, being necessary to peace, and depending on sovereign power, is the act of that power, in order to the public peace. These rules of propriety, or meum and tuum, and of good, evil, lawful, and unlawful in the actions of subjects, are the civil laws; that is to say, the laws of each commonwealth in particular; though the name of civil law be now restrained to the ancient civil laws of the city of Rome; which being the head of a great part of

the world, her laws at that time were in these parts the
civil law.

To him also belongeth the right of judicature and decision of controversy.

Eightly, is annexed to the sovereignty, the right of judicature; that is to say, of hearing and deciding all controversies, which may arise concerning law, either civil, or
natural; or concerning fact. For without the decision of
controversies, there is no protection of one subject,
against the injuries of another; the laws concerning
meum and tuum are in vain; and to every man remaineth,
from the natural and necessary appetite of his own conservation, the right of protecting himself by his private
strength, which is the condition of war, and contrary to
the end for which every commonwealth is instituted.

And of making war, and peace, as he shall think best.

Ninthly, is annexed to the sovereignty, the right of
making war and peace with other nations, and commonwealths; that is to say, of judging when it is for
the public good, and how great forces are to be assembled, armed, and paid for that end; and to levy money
upon the subjects, to defray the expenses thereof. For
the power by which the people are to be defended,
consisteth in their armies; and the strength of an
army, in the union of their strength under one com-

mand; which command the sovereign instituted, therefore hath; because the command of the militia, without other institution, maketh him that hath it sovereign. And therefore whosoever is made general of an army, he that hath the sovereign power is always generalissimo.

And of choosing all counsellors and ministers, both of peace & war.

Tenthly, is annexed to the sovereignty, the choosing of all counsellors, ministers, magistrates, and officers, both in peace, and war. For seeing the sovereign is charged with the end, which is the common peace and defence, he is understood to have power to use such means, as he shall think most fit for his discharge.

And of rewarding and punishing, and that (where no former law hath determined the measure of it) arbitrarily.

Eleventhly, to the sovereign is committed the power of rewarding with riches, or honour, and of punishing with corporal or pecuniary punishment, or with ignominy, every subject according to the law he hath formerly made; or if there be no law made, according as he shall judge most to conduce to the encouraging of men to serve the commonwealth, or deterring of them from doing disservice to the same.

AND OF HONOUR AND ORDER.

Lastly, considering what value men are naturally apt to set upon themselves; what respect they look for from others; and how little they value other men; from whence continually arise amongst them, emulation, quarrels, factions, and at last war, to the destroying of one another, and diminution of their strength against a common enemy; it is necessary that there be laws of honour, and a public rate of the worth of such men as have deserved, or are able to deserve well of the commonwealth; and that there be force in the hands of some or other, to put those laws in execution. But it hath already been shown, that not only the whole militia, or forces of the commonwealth; but also the judicature of all controversies, is annexed to the sovereignty. To the sovereign therefore it belongeth also to give titles of honour; and to appoint what order of place, and dignity, each man shall hold; and what signs of respect, in public or private meetings, they shall give to one another.

THESE RIGHTS ARE INDIVISIBLE.

These are the rights, which make the essence of sovereignty; and which are the marks, whereby a man may discern in what man, or assembly of men, the sovereign power is placed, and resideth. For these are incommunicable, and inseparable. The power to coin money; to dispose of the estate and persons of infant heirs; to have

præemption in markets; and all other statute preroga-
tives, may be transferred by the sovereign; and yet the
power to protect his subjects be retained. But if he transfer the militia, he retains the judicature in vain, for want
of execution of the laws: or if he grant away the power of
raising money; the militia is in vain; or if he give away
the government of doctrines, men will be frighted into
rebellion with the fear of spirits. And so if we consider
any one of the said rights, we shall presently see, that
the holding of all the rest will produce no effect, in the
conservation of peace and justice, the end for which
all commonwealths are instituted. And this division is
it, whereof it is said, a kingdom divided in itself cannot
stand: for unless this division precede, division into
opposite armies can never happen. If there had not first
been an opinion received of the greatest part of England,
that these powers were divided between the King, and the
Lords, and the House of Commons, the people had never
been divided and fallen into this civil war; first between
those that disagreed in politics; and after between the
dissenters about the liberty of religion; which have so
instructed men in this point of sovereign right, that there
be few now in England that do not see, that these rights
are inseparable, and will be so generally acknowledged at
the next return of peace; and so continue, till their miseries are forgotten; and no longer, except the vulgar be better taught than they have hitherto been.

AND CAN BY NO GRANT PASS AWAY WITHOUT
DIRECT RENOUNCING OF THE SOVEREIGN POWER.

And because they are essential and inseparable rights, it follows necessarily, that in whatsoever words any of them seem to be granted away, yet if the sovereign power itself be not in direct terms renounced, and the name of sovereign no more given by the grantees to him that grants them, the grant is void: for when he has granted all he can, if we grant back the sovereignty, all is restored, as inseparably annexed thereunto.

THE POWER AND HONOUR OF SUBJECTS VANISHETH
IN THE PRESENCE OF THE POWER SOVEREIGN.

This great authority being indivisible, and inseparably annexed to the sovereignty, there is little ground for the opinion of them, that say of sovereign kings, though they be *singulis majores*, of greater power than every one of their subjects, yet they be *universis minores*, of less power than them all together. For if by all together, they mean not the collective body as one person, then all together, and every one, signify the same; and the speech is absurd. But if by all together, they understand them as one person, which person the sovereign bears, then the power of all together, is the same with the sovereign's power; and so again the speech is absurd: which absurdity they see well enough, when the sovereignty is in an assembly of the people; but in a monarch they see it not;

and yet the power of sovereignty is the same in whomsoever it be placed.

And as the power, so also the honour of the sovereign, ought to be greater, than that of any, or all the
subjects. For in the sovereignty is the fountain of honour. The dignities of lord, earl, duke, and prince are his
creatures. As in the presence of the master, the servants
are equal, and without any honour at all; so are the subjects, in the presence of the sovereign. And though they
shine some more, some less, when they are out of his
sight; yet in his presence, they shine no more than the
stars in the presence of the sun.

Sovereign power not so hurtful as the want of it, and the hurt proceeds for the greatest part from not submitting readily to a less.

But a man may here object, that the condition of subjects is very miserable; as being obnoxious to the lusts,
and other irregular passions of him, or them that
have so unlimited a power in their hands. And commonly they that live under a monarch, think it the
fault of monarchy; and they that live under the government of democracy, or other sovereign assembly,
attribute all the inconvenience to that form of commonwealth; whereas the power in all forms, if they be
perfect enough to protect them, is the same: not con-

sidering that the state of man can never be without
some incommodity or other; and that the greatest,
that in any form of government can possibly happen
to the people in general, is scarce sensible, in respect
of the miseries, and horrible calamities, that accom-
pany a civil war, or that dissolute condition of masterless men, without subjection to laws, and a coercive
power to tie their hands from rapine and revenge: nor
considering that the greatest pressure of sovereign
governors, proceedeth not from any delight, or profit
they can expect in the damage or weakening of their
subjects, in whose vigour, consisteth their own
strength and glory; but in the restiveness of themselves, that unwillingly contributing to their own
defence, make it necessary for their governors to draw
from them what they can in time of peace, that they
may have means on any emergent occasion, or sudden
need, to resist, or take advantage on their enemies.
For all men are by nature provided of notable multi-
plying glasses, that is their passions and self-love,
through which, every little payment appeareth a great
grievance; but are destitute of those prospective
glasses, namely moral and civil science, to see afar off
the miseries that hang over them, and cannot without
such payments be avoided.

CHAPTER XIX

OF THE SEVERAL KINDS OF COMMONWEALTH BY INSTITUTION, AND OF SUCCESSION TO THE SOVEREIGN POWER

THE DIFFERENT FORMS OF COMMONWEALTHS BUT THREE.
The difference of commonwealths, consisteth in the difference of the sovereign, or the person representative of all and every one of the multitude. And because the sovereignty is either in one man, or in an assembly of more than one; and into that assembly either every man hath right to enter, or not every one, but certain men distinguished from the rest; it is manifest, there can be but three kinds of commonwealth. For the representative must needs be one man, or more: and if more, then it is the assembly of all, or but of a part. When the representative is one man, then is the commonwealth a monarchy: when an assembly of all that will come together, then it is a democracy, or popular commonwealth: when an assembly of a a part only, then it is called an aristocracy. Other kind of commonwealth there can be none: for either one, or more, or all, must have the sovereign power, which I have shown to be indivisible, entire.

TYRANNY AND OLIGARCHY, BUT DIFFERENT NAMES OF MONARCHY, AND ARISTOCRACY.

There be other names of government, in the histories, and books of policy; as tyranny, and oligarchy: but they are not the names of other forms of government, but of the same forms misliked. For they that are discontented under monarchy, call it tyranny; and they that are displeased with aristocracy, call it oligarchy: so also, they which find themselves grieved under a democracy, call it anarchy, which signifies want of government; and yet I think no man believes, that want of government, is any new kind of government: nor by the same reason ought they to believe, that the government is of one kind, when they like it, and another, when they mislike it, or are oppressed by the governors.

SUBORDINATE REPRESENTATIVES DANGEROUS.

It is manifest, that men who are in absolute liberty, may, if they please, give authority to one man, to represent them every one; as well as give such authority to any assembly of men whatsoever; and consequently may subject themselves, if they think good, to a monarch, as absolutely, as to any other representative. Therefore, where there is already erected a sovereign power, there can be no other representative of the same people, but only to certain particular ends, by the sovereign lim-

ited. For that were to erect two sovereigns; and every
man to have his person represented by two actors, that
by opposing one another, must needs divide that power,
which, if men will live in peace, is indivisible; and
thereby reduce the multitude into the condition of war,
contrary to the end for which all sovereignty is instituted. And therefore as it is absurd, to think that a
sovereign assembly, inviting the people of their dominion, to send up their deputies, with power to make
known their advice, or desires, should therefore hold
such deputies, rather than themselves, for the absolute
representatives of the people: so it is absurd also, to
think the same in a monarchy. And I know not how
this so manifest a truth, should of late be so little
observed; that in a monarchy, he that had the sovereignty from a descent of six hundred years, was alone
called sovereign, had the title of Majesty from every
one of his subjects, and was unquestionably taken by
them for their king, was notwithstanding never considered as their representative; the name without contradiction passing for the title of those men, which at his
command were sent up by the people to carry their
petitions, and give him, if he permitted it, their advice.
Which may serve as an admonition, for those that are
the true, and absolute representative of a people, to
instruct men in the nature of that office, and to take
heed how they admit of any other general representa-

tion upon any occasion whatsoever, if they mean to discharge the trust committed to them.

COMPARISON OF MONARCHY, WITH SOVEREIGN ASSEMBLIES.

The difference between these three kinds of commonwealth, consisteth not in the difference of power; but in
the difference of convenience, or aptitude to produce
the peace, and security of the people; for which end they
were instituted. And to compare monarchy with the
other two, we may observe; first, that whosoever beareth
the person of the people, or is one of that assembly that
bears it, beareth also his own natural person. And
though he be careful in his politic person to procure the
common interest; yet he is more, or no less careful to
procure the private good of himself, his family, kindred
and friends; and for the most part, if the public interest
chance to cross the private, he prefers the private: for
the passions of men, are commonly more potent than
their reason. From whence it follows, that where the
public and private interest are most closely united, there
is the public most advanced. Now in monarchy, the private interest is the same with the public. The riches,
power, and honour of a monarch arise only from the
riches, strength and reputation of his subjects. For no
king can be rich, nor glorious, nor secure, whose subjects are either poor, or contemptible, or too weak
through want or dissention, to maintain a war against

their enemies: whereas in a democracy, or aristocracy, the public prosperity confers not so much to the private fortune of one that is corrupt, or ambitious, as doth many times a perfidious advice, a treacherous action, or a civil war.

Secondly, that a monarch receiveth counsel of whom, when, and where he pleaseth; and consequently may hear the opinion of men versed in the matter about which he deliberates, of what rank or quality soever, and as long before the time of action, and with as much secrecy, as he will. But when a sovereign assembly has need of counsel, none are admitted but such as have a right thereto from the beginning; which for the most part are of those who have been versed more in the acquisition of wealth than of knowledge; and are to give their advice in long discourses, which may, and do commonly excite men to action, but not govern them in it. For the understanding is by the flame of the passions, never enlightened, but dazzled. Nor is there any place, or time, wherein an assembly can receive counsel with secrecy, because of their own multitude.

Thirdly, that the resolutions of a monarch, are subject to no other inconstancy, than that of human nature; but in assemblies, besides that of nature, there ariseth an inconstancy from the number. For the absence of a few, that would have the resolution once taken, continue firm, which may happen by security, negligence, or pri-

vate impediments, or the diligent appearance of a few of
the contrary opinion, undoes to-day, all that was concluded yesterday.

Fourthly, that a monarch cannot disagree with himself, out of envy, or interest; but an assembly may; and
that to such a height, as may produce a civil war.

Fifthly, that in monarchy there is this inconvenience;
that any subject, by the power of one man, for the
enriching of a favourite or flatterer, may be deprived of
all he possesseth; which I confess is a great and inevi-
table inconvenience. But the same may as well happen,
where the sovereign power is in an assembly: for their
power is the same; and they are as subject to evil counsel, and to be seduced by orators, as a monarch by flatterers; and becoming one another's flatterers, serve one
another's covetousness and ambition by turns. And
whereas the favourites of monarchs, are few, and they
have none else to advance but their own kindred; the
favourites of an assembly, are many; and the kindred
much more numerous, than of any monarch. Besides,
there is no favourite of a monarch, which cannot as well
succour his friends, as hurt his enemies: but orators,
that is to say, favourites of sovereign assemblies, though
they have great power to hurt, have little to save. For to
accuse, requires less eloquence, such is man's nature,
than to excuse; and condemnation, than absolution
more resembles justice.

Sixthly, that it is an inconvenience in monarchy, that the sovereignty may descend upon an infant, or one that cannot discern between good and evil: and consisteth in this, that the use of his power, must be in the hand of another man, or of some assembly of men, which are to govern by his right, and in his name; as curators, and protectors of his person, and authority. But to say there is inconvenience, in putting the use of the sovereign power, into the hand of a man, or an assembly of men; is to say that all government is more inconvenient, than confusion, and civil war. And therefore all the danger that can be pretended, must arise from the contention of those, that for an office of so great honour, and profit, may become competitors. To make it appear, that this inconvenience, proceedeth not from that form of government we call monarchy, we are to consider, that the precedent monarch hath appointed who shall have the tuition of his infant successor, either expressly by testament, or tacitly, by not controlling the custom in that case received: and then such inconvenience, if it happen, is to be attributed, not to the monarchy, but to the ambition, and injustice of the subjects; which in all kinds of government, where the people are not well instructed in their duty, and the rights of sovereignty, is the same. Or else the precedent monarch hath not at all taken order for such tuition; and then the law of nature hath provided this sufficient rule, that the tuition shall be in him, that hath by nature most interest in the preservation of the authority of the infant, and to whom least benefit can accrue by his death, or diminution. For seeing every man by nature seeketh his own benefit, and promotion; to put an infant into the power of those, that can promote themselves by his destruction, or damage, is not tuition, but treachery. So that sufficient provision being taken, against all just quarrel, about the government under a child, if any contention arise to the disturbance of the public peace, it is not to be attributed to the form of monarchy, but to the ambition of subjects, and ignorance of their duty. On the other side, there is no great commonwealth, the sovereignty whereof is in a great assembly, which is not, as to consultations of peace, and war, and making of laws, in the same condition, as if the government were in a child. For as a child wants the judgment to dissent from counsel given him, and is thereby necessitated to take the advice of them, or him, to whom he is committed: so an assembly wanteth the liberty, to dissent from the counsel of the major part, be it good, or bad. And as a child has need of a tutor, or protector, to preserve his person and authority: so also, in great commonwealths, the sovereign assembly, in all great dangers and troubles, have need of custodes libertatis; that is of dictators, or protectors of their authority; which are as much as temporary monarchs, to whom for a time, they may commit the entire exercise of their power; and have, at the end of that time, been oftener deprived thereof, than infant kings, by their protectors, regents, or any other tutors.

DEFINITION OF MONARCHY, AND OTHER FORMS.

Though the kinds of sovereignty be, as I have now shown, but three; that is to say, monarchy, where one man has it; or democracy, where the general assembly of subjects hath it; or aristocracy, where it is in an assembly of certain persons nominated, or otherwise distinguished from the rest: yet he that shall consider the particular commonwealths that have been, and are in the world, will not perhaps easily reduce them to three, and may thereby be inclined to think there be other forms, arising from these mingled together. As for example, elective kingdoms; where kings have the sovereign power put into their hands for a time; or kingdoms, wherein the king hath a power limited: which governments, are nevertheless by most writers called monarchy. Likewise if a popular, or aristocratical commonwealth, subdue an enemy's country, and govern the same, by a president, procurator, or other magistrate; this may seem perhaps at first sight, to be a democratical, or aristocratical government. But it is not so. For elective kings, are not sovereigns, but ministers of the sovereign; nor limited kings, sovereigns, but ministers of them that have the sovereign power: nor are those provinces which are in subjection to a democracy, or aristrocracy of another commonwealth, democratically or aristocratically governed, but monarchically.

Definition of monarchy, &c.

And first, concerning an elective king, whose power is limited to his life, as it is in many places of Christendom at this day; or to certain years or months, as the dictator's power amongst the Romans; if he have right to appoint his successor, he is no more elective but hereditary. But if he have no power to elect his successor, then there is some other man, or assembly known, which after his decease may elect anew, or else the commonwealth dieth, and dissolveth with him, and returneth to the condition of war. If it be known who have the power to give the sovereignty after his death, it is known also that the sovereignty was in them before: for none have right to give that which they have not right to possess, and keep to themselves, if they think good. But if there be none that can give the sovereignty, after the decease of him that was first elected; then has he power, nay he is obliged by the law of nature, to provide, by establishing his successor, to keep those that had trusted him with the government, from relapsing into the miserable condition of civil war. And consequently he was, when elected, a sovereign absolute.

Secondly, that king whose power is limited, is not

superior to him, or them that have the power to limit it; and he that is not superior, is not supreme; that is to say not sovereign. The sovereignty therefore was always in that assembly which had the right to limit him; and by consequence the government not monarchy, but either democracy, or aristocracy; as of old time in Sparta; where the kings had a privilege to lead their armies; but the sovereignty was in the Ephori.

Thirdly, whereas heretofore the Roman people governed the land of Judea, for example, by a president; yet was not Judea therefore a democracy; because they were not governed by any assembly, into the which, any of them, had right to enter; nor an aristocracy; because they were not governed by any assembly, into which, any man could enter by their election: but they were governed by one person, which, though as to the people of Rome, was an assembly of the people, or democracy; yet as to the people of Judea, which had no right at all of participating in the government, was a monarch. For though where the people are governed by an assembly, chosen by themselves out of their own number, the government is called a democracy, or aristocracy; yet when they are governed by an assembly, not of their own choosing, it is a monarchy; not of one man, over another man; but of one people, over another people.

OF THE RIGHT OF SUCCESSION.

Of all these forms of government, the matter being mortal, so that not only monarchs, but also whole assemblies die, it is necessary for the conservation of the peace of men, that as there was order taken for an artificial man, so there be order also taken, for an artificial eternity of life; without which, men that are governed by an assembly, should return into the condition of war in every age; and they that are governed by one man, as soon as their governor dieth. This artificial eternity, is that which men call the right of succession.

There is no perfect form of government, where the disposing of the succession is not in the present sovereign. For if it be in any other particular man, or private assembly, it is in a person subject, and may be assumed by the sovereign at his pleasure; and consequently the right is in himself. And if it be in no particular man, but left to a new choice; then is the commonwealth dissolved; and the right is in him that can get it; contrary to the intention of them that did institute the commonwealth, for their perpetual, and not temporary security.

In a democracy, the whole assembly cannot fail, unless the multitude that are to be governed fail. And therefore questions of the right of succession, have in that form of government no place at all.

In an aristocracy, when any of the assembly dieth, the election of another into his room belongeth to the assembly, as the sovereign, to whom belongeth the choosing of all counsellors and officers. For that which the representative doth, as actor, every one of the subjects doth, as author. And though the sovereign assembly may give power to others, to elect new men, for supply of their court; yet it is still by their authority, that the election is made; and by the same it may, when the public shall require it, be recalled.

THE PRESENT MONARCH HATH RIGHT
TO DISPOSE OF THE SUCCESSION.

The greatest difficulty about the right of succession, is in monarchy: and the difficulty ariseth from this, that at first sight, it is not manifest who is to appoint the successor; nor many times, who it is whom he hath appointed. For in both these cases, there is required a more exact ratiocination, than every man is accustomed to use. As to the question, who shall appoint the successor, of a monarch that hath the sovereign authority; that is to say, who shall determine of the right of inheritance, (for elective kings and princes have not the sovereign power in propriety, but in use only), we are to consider, that either he that is in possession, has right to dispose of the succession, or else that right is again in the dissolved multitude. For the death of him that

hath the sovereign power in propriety, leaves the multitude without any sovereign at all; that is, without any
representative in whom they should be united, and be
capable of doing any one action at all: and therefore
they are incapable of election of any new monarch;
every man having equal right to submit himself to
such as he thinks best able to protect him; or if he
can, protect himself by his own sword; which is a
return to confusion, and to the condition of a war of
every man against every man, contrary to the end for
which monarchy had its first institution. Therefore it
is manifest, that by the institution of monarchy, the
disposing of the successor, is always left to the judgment and will of the present possessor.

And for the question, which may arise sometimes,
who it is that the monarch in possession, hath designed
to the succession and inheritance of his power; it is
determined by his express words, and testament; or by
other tacit signs sufficient.

Succession passeth by express words.

By express words, or testament, when it is declared by
him in his lifetime, viva voce, or by writing; as the first
emperors of Rome declared who should be their heirs.
For the word heir does not of itself imply the children,
or nearest kindred of a man; but whomsoever a man
shall any way declare, he would have to succeed him in

his estate. If therefore a monarch declare expressly, that
such a man shall be his heir, either by word or writing,
then is that man immediately after the decease of his
predecessor, invested in the right of being monarch.

Or, by not controlling a custom.

But where testament, and express words are wanting,
other natural signs of the will are to be followed:
whereof the one is custom. And therefore where the
custom is, that the next of kindred absolutely succeedeth, there also the next of kindred hath right to the
succession; for that, if the will of him that was in possession had been otherwise, he might easily have declared
the same in his life-time. And likewise where the custom is, that the next of the male kindred succeedeth,
there also the right of succession is in the next of the
kindred male, for the same reason. And so it is if the
custom were to advance the female. For whatsoever custom a man may by a word control, and does not, it is a
natural sign he would have that custom stand.

Or, by presumption of natural affection.

But where neither custom, nor testament hath preceded,
there it is to be understood, first, that a monarch's will
is, that the government remain monarchical; because he
hath approved that government in himself. Secondly,
that a child of his own, male, or female, be preferred

before any other; because men are presumed to be more inclined by nature, to advance their own children, than the children of other men; and of their own, rather a male than a female; because men, are naturally fitter than women, for actions of labour and danger. Thirdly, where his own issue faileth, rather a brother than a stranger; and so still the nearer in blood, rather than the more remote; because it is always presumed that the nearer of kin, is the nearer in affection; and it is evident that a man receives always, by reflection, the most honour from the greatness of his nearest kindred.

To DISPOSE OF THE SUCCESSION, THOUGH TO A KING OF ANOTHER NATION, NOT UNLAWFUL.

But if it be lawful for a monarch to dispose of the succession by words of contract, or testament, men may perhaps object a great inconvenience: for he may sell, or give his right of governing to a stranger; which, because strangers, that is, men not used to live under the same government, nor speaking the same language, do commonly undervalue one another, may turn to the oppression of his subjects; which is indeed a great inconvenience: but it proceedeth not necessarily from the subjection to a stranger's government, but from the unskilfulness of the governors, ignorant of the true rules of politics. And therefore the Romans when they had subdued many nations, to make their government digestible, were wont to take away that grievance, as much as they thought necessary, by giving sometimes to whole nations, and sometimes to principal men of every nation they conquered, not only the privileges, but also the name of Romans; and took many of them into the senate, and offices of charge, even in the Roman city. And this was it our most wise king, king James, aimed at, in endeavouring the union of his two realms of England and Scotland. Which if he could have obtained, had in all likelihood prevented the civil wars, which make both those kingdoms, at this present, miserable. It is not therefore any injury to the people, for a monarch to dispose of the succession by will; though by the fault of many princes, it hath been sometimes found inconvenient. Of the lawfulness of it, this also is an argument, that whatsoever inconvenience can arrive by giving a kingdom to a stranger, may arrive also by so marrying with strangers, as the right of succession may descend upon them: yet this by all men is accounted lawful.

CHAPTER XX

OF DOMINION PATERNAL, AND DESPOTICAL

A COMMONWEALTH BY ACQUISITION.

A commonwealth by acquisition, is that, where the sovereign power is acquired by force; and it is acquired by force, when men singly, or many together by plurality of voices, for fear of death, or bonds, do authorize all the actions of that man, or assembly, that hath their lives and liberty in his power.

WHEREIN DIFFERENT FROM A COMMONWEALTH BY INSTITUTION.

And this kind of dominion, or sovereignty, differeth from sovereignty by institution, only in this, that men who choose their sovereign, do it for fear of one another, and not of him whom they institute: but in this case, they subject themselves, to him they are afraid of. In both cases they do it for fear: which is to be noted by them, that hold all such covenants, as proceed from fear of death or violence, void: which if it were true, no man, in any kind of commonwealth, could be obliged to obedience. It is true, that in a commonwealth once instituted, or acquired, promises proceeding from fear of death or violence, are no covenants, nor obliging, when the thing promised is contrary to the laws; but the reason is not, because it was made upon fear, but because he that promiseth, hath no right in the thing promised. Also, when he may lawfully perform, and doth not, it is not the invalidity of the covenant, that absolveth him, but the sentence of the sovereign. Otherwise, whensoever a man lawfully promiseth, he unlawfully breaketh: but when the sovereign, who is the actor, acquitteth him, then he is acquitted by him that extorted the promise, as by the author of such absolution.

THE RIGHTS OF SOVEREIGNTY THE SAME IN BOTH.

But the rights, and consequences of sovereignty, are the same in both. His power cannot, without his consent, be transferred to another: he cannot forfeit it: he cannot be accused by any of his subjects, of injury: he cannot be punished by them: he is judge of what is necessary for peace; and judge of doctrines: he is sole legislator; and supreme judge of controversies; and of the times, and occasions of war, and peace: to him it belongeth to choose magistrates, counsellors, commanders, and all other officers, and ministers; and to determine of rewards, and punishments, honour, and order. The reasons whereof, are the same which are alleged in the precedent chapter, for the same rights, and consequences of sovereignty by institution.

DOMINION PATERNAL HOW ATTAINED.

NOT BY GENERATION, BUT BY CONTRACT.

Dominion is acquired two ways; by generation, and by conquest. The right of dominion by generation, is that, which the parent hath over his children; and is called paternal. And is not so derived from the generation, as if therefore the parent had dominion over his child because he begat him; but from the child's consent, either express, or by other sufficient arguments declared. For as to the generation, God hath ordained to man a helper; and there be always two that are equally parents: the dominion therefore over the child, should belong equally to both; and he be equally subject to both, which is impossible; for no man can obey two masters. And whereas some have attributed the dominion to the man only, as being of the more excellent sex; they misreckon in it. For there is not always that difference of strength, or prudence between the man and the woman, as that the right can be determined without war. In commonwealths, this controversy is decided by the civil law; and for the most part, but not always, the sentence is in favour of the father; because for the most part commonwealths have been erected by the fathers, not by the mothers of families. But the question lieth now in the state of mere nature; where there are supposed no laws of matrimony; no laws for the education of children; but the law of nature, and the natural inclination of the sexes, one to another, and to their children. In this condition of mere nature, either the parents between themselves dispose of the dominion over the child by contract; or do not dispose thereof at all. If they dispose thereof, the right passeth according to the contract. We find in history that the Amazons contracted with the men of the neighbouring countries, to whom they had recourse for issue, that the issue male should be sent back, but the female remain with themselves: so that the dominion of the females was in the mother.

Or education.

If there be no contract, the dominion is in the mother. For in the condition of mere nature, where there are no matrimonial laws, it cannot be known who is the father, unless it be declared by the mother: and therefore the right of dominion over the child dependeth on her will, and is consequently hers. Again, seeing the infant is first in the power of the mother, so as she may either nourish, or expose it; if she nourish it, it oweth its life to the mother; and is therefore obliged to obey her, rather than any other; and by consequence the dominion over it is hers. But if she expose it, and another find and nourish it, the dominion is in him that nourisheth it. For it ought to obey him by whom it is preserved; because preservation of life being the end, for which one man becomes subject to another, every man is supposed to promise obedience, to him, in whose power it is to save, or destroy him.

Or precedent subjection of one of the parents to the other.

If the mother be the father's subject, the child, is in the father's power: and if the father be the mother's subject, as when a sovereign queen marrieth one of her subjects, the child is subject to the mother; because the father also is her subject.

If a man and woman, monarchs of two several kingdoms, have a child, and contract concerning who shall have the dominion of him, the right of the dominion passeth by the contract. If they contract not, the dominion followeth the dominion of the place of his residence. For the sovereign of each country hath dominion over all that reside therein.

He that hath the dominion over the child, hath dominion also over the children of the child; and over their children's children. For he that hath dominion over the person of a man, hath dominion over all that is his; without which, dominion were but a title, without the effect.

THE RIGHT OF SUCCESSION FOLLOWETH
THE RULES OF THE RIGHT OF POSSESSION.

The right of succession to paternal dominion, proceedeth in the same manner, as doth the right of succession of monarchy; of which I have already sufficiently spoken in the precedent chapter.

DESPOTICAL DOMINION ATTAINED.

Dominion acquired by conquest, or victory in war, is that which some writers call despotical, from Δεσπόστης, which signifieth a lord, or master; and is the dominion of the master over his servant. And this dominion is then acquired to the victor, when the vanquished, to avoid the present stroke of death, covenan-

teth either in express words, or by other sufficient
signs of the will, that so long as his life, and the liberty of his body is allowed him, the victor shall have
the use thereof, at his pleasure. And after such covenant made, the vanquished is a servant, and not before:
for by the word servant, whether it be derived from
servire, to serve, or from *servare*, to save, which I leave to
grammarians to dispute, is not meant a captive, which
is kept in prison, or bonds, till the owner of him that
took him, or bought him of one that did, shall consider what to do with him: for such men, commonly
called slaves, have no obligation at all; but may break
their bonds, or the prison; and kill, or carry away captive their master, justly: but one, that being taken,
hath corporal liberty allowed him; and upon promise
not to run away, nor to do violence to his master, is
trusted by him.

Not by the victory, but by
the consent of the vanquished.

It is not therefore the victory, that giveth the right of
dominion over the vanquished, but his own covenant.
Nor is he obliged because he is conquered; that is to say,
beaten, and taken, or put to flight; but because he
cometh in, and submitteth to the victor; nor is the victor obliged by an enemy's rendering himself, without
promise of life, to spare him for this his yielding to

discretion; which obliges not the victor longer, than in
his own discretion he shall think fit.

And that which men do, when they demand, as it is
now called, quarter, which the Greeks called Ζωγρία,
taking alive, is to evade the present fury of the victor,
by submission, and to compound for their life, with
ransom, or service: and therefore he that hath quarter,
hath not his life given, but deferred till farther deliberation; for it is not a yielding on condition of life, but
to discretion. And then only is his life in security, and
his service due, when the victor hath trusted him with
his corporal liberty. For slaves that work in prisons; or
fetters, do it not of duty, but to avoid the cruelty of
their task-masters.

The master of the servant, is master also of all he
hath: and may exact the use thereof; that is to say, of his
goods, of his labour, of his servants, and of his children,
as often as he shall think fit. For he holdeth his life of
his master, by the covenant of obedience; that is, of
owning, and authorizing whatsoever the master shall
do. And in case the master, if he refuse, kill him, or cast
him into bonds, or otherwise punish him for his disobedience, he is himself the author of the same; and
cannot accuse him of injury.

In sum, the rights and consequences of both paternal and despotical dominion, are the very same with
those of a sovereign by institution; and for the same

reasons: which reasons are set down in the precedent chapter. So that for a man that is monarch of divers nations, whereof he hath, in one the sovereignty by institution of the people assembled, and in another by conquest, that is by the submission of each particular, to avoid death or bonds; to demand of one nation more than of the other, from the title of conquest, as being a conquered nation, is an act of ignorance of the rights of sovereignty; for the sovereign is absolute over both alike; or else there is no sovereignty at all; and so every man may lawfully protect himself, if he can, with his own sword, which is the condition of war.

Difference between a family and a kingdom.

By this it appears; that a great family, if it be not part of some commonwealth, is of itself, as to the rights of sovereignty, a little monarchy: whether that family consist of a man and his children; or of a man and his servants; or of a man, and his children, and servants together: wherein the father or master is the sovereign. But yet a family is not properly a commonwealth; unless it be of that power by its own number, or by other opportunities, as not to be subdued without the hazard of war. for where a number of men are manifestly too weak to defend themselves united, every one may use his own reason in time of danger, to save his own life, either by flight, or by submission to the enemy, as he shall think best; in the same manner as a very small company of soldiers, surprised by an army, may cast down their arms, and demand quarter, or run away, rather than be put to the sword. And thus much shall suffice, concerning what I find by speculation, and deduction, of sovereign rights, from the nature, need, and designs of men, in erecting of commonwealths, and putting themselves under monarchs, or assemblies, entrusted with power enough for their protection.

THE RIGHTS OF MONARCHY FROM SCRIPTURE.

Let us now consider what the Scripture teacheth in the same point. To Moses, the children of Israel say thus: Speak thou to us, and we will hear thee; but let not God speak to us, lest we die. (Exod. xx. 19.) This is absolute obedience to Moses. Concerning the right of kings, God himself by the mouth of Samuel, saith, (I Sam. viii. 11, 12, &c.) This shall be the right of the king you will have to reign over you. He shall take your sons, and set them to drive his chariots, and to be his horsemen, and to run before his chariots; and gather in his harvest; and to make his engines of war, and instruments of his chariots; and shall take your daughters to make perfumes, to be his cooks, and bakers. He shall take your fields, your vine-yards, and your olive-yards, and give them to his servants. He shall take the tithe of your corn and wine, and give it to the men of his chamber,

and to his other servants. He shall take your man-
servants, and your maid-servants, and the choice of
your youth, and employ them in his business. He shall
take the tithe of your flocks; and you shall be his servants. This is absolute power, and summed up in the
last words, you shall be his servants. Again, when the
people heard what power their king was to have, yet
they consented thereto, and say thus, (verse 10) we will
be as all other nations, and our king shall judge our
causes, and go before us, to conduct our wars. Here is
confirmed the right that sovereigns have, both to the
militia, and to all judicature; in which is contained as
absolute power, as one man can possibly transfer to
another. Again, the prayer of king Solomon to God, was
this (I Kings, iii. 9): Give to thy servant understanding,
to judge thy people, and to discern between good and
evil. It belongeth therefore to the sovereign to be judge,
and to prescribe the rules of discerning good and evil:
which rules are laws; and therefore in him is the legislative power. Saul sought the life of David; yet when it
was in his power to slay Saul, and his servants would
have done it, David forbad them, saying, (I Sam. xxiv.
6) God forbid I should do such an act against my Lord,
the anointed of God. For obedience of servants St. Paul
saith; (Col. iii. 22) Servants obey your masters in all
things; and, (Col. iii. 20) children obey your parents in
all things. There is simple obedience in those that are

subject to paternal, or despotical dominion. Again, (Matt. xxiii. 2, 3) The Scribes and Pharisees sit in Moses' chair, and therefore all that they shall bid you observe, that observe and do. There again is simple obedience. And St. Paul, (Titus iii. 2) Warn them that they subject themselves to princes, and to those that are in authority, and obey them. This obedience is also simple. Lastly, our Saviour himself acknowledges, that men ought to pay such taxes as are by kings imposed, where he says, give to Cæsar that which is Cæsar's; and paid such taxes himself. And that the king's word, is sufficient to take anything from any subject, when there is need; and that the king is judge of that need: for he himself, as king of the Jews, commanded his disciples to take the ass, and ass's colt to carry him into Jerusalem, saying, (Matth. xxi. 2, 3) Go into the village over against you, and you shall find a she ass tied, and her colt with her, untie them, and bring them to me. And if any man ask you, what you mean by it, say the Lord hath need of them: and they will let them go. They will not ask whether his necessity be a sufficient title; nor whether he be judge of that necessity; but acquiesce in the will of the Lord.

To these places may be added also that of Genesis, (iii. 5) Ye shall be as gods, knowing good and evil. And (verse 11) Who told thee that thou wast naked? hast thou eaten of the tree, of which I commanded thee thou shouldest not eat? For the cognizance or judicature of good and evil, being forbidden by the name of the fruit of the tree of knowledge, as a trial of Adam's obedience; the devil to inflame the ambition of the woman, to whom that fruit already seemed beautiful, told her that by tasting it, they should be as gods, knowing good and evil. Whereupon having both eaten, they did indeed take upon them God's office, which is judicature of good and evil; but acquired no new ability to distinguish between them aright. And whereas it is said, that having eaten, they saw they were naked; no man hath so interpreted that place, as if they had been formerly blind, and saw not their own skins: the meaning is plain, that it was then they first judged their nakedness, wherein it was God's will to create them, to be uncomely; and by being ashamed, did tacitly censure God himself. And thereupon God saith; Hast thou eaten, &c. as if he should say, doest thou that owest me obedience, take upon thee to judge of my commandments? Whereby it is clearly, though allegorically, signified, that the commands of them that have the right to command, are not by their subjects to be censured, nor disputed.

Sovereign power ought in all commonwealths to be absolute.

So that it appeareth plainly, to my understanding, both from reason, and Scripture, that the sovereign power, whether placed in one man, as in monarchy, or in one assembly of men, as in popular, and aristocratical commonwealths, is as great, as possibly men can be imagined to make it. And though of so unlimited a power, men may fancy many evil consequences, yet the consequences of the want of it, which is perpetual war of every man against his neighbour, are much worse. The condition of man in this life shall never be without inconveniences; but there happeneth in no commonwealth any great inconvenience, but what proceeds from the subject's disobedience, and breach of those covenants, from which the commonwealth hath its being. And whosoever thinking sovereign power too great, will seek to make it less, must subject himself, to the power, that can limit it; that is to say, to a greater.

The greatest objection is, that of the practice; when men ask, where, and when, such power has by subjects been acknowledged. But one may ask them again, when, or where has there been a kingdom long free from sedition and civil war. In those nations, whose commonwealths have been long-lived, and not been destroyed but by foreign war, the subjects never did dispute of the sovereign power. But howsoever, an argument from the practice of men, that have not sifted to the bottom, and with exact reason weighed the causes, and nature of commonwealths, and suffer daily those miseries, that proceed from the ignorance thereof, is invalid. For though in all places of the world, men should lay the foundation of their houses on the sand, it could not thence be inferred, that so it ought to be. The skill of making, and maintaining commonwealths, consisteth in certain rules, as doth arithmetic and geometry; not, as tennis-play, on practice only: which rules, neither poor men have the leisure, nor men that have had the leisure, have hitherto had the curiosity, or the method to find out.

CHAPTER XXI

OF THE LIBERTY OF SUBJECTS

LIBERTY WHAT.

Liberty, or freedom, signifieth, properly, the absence of opposition; by opposition, I mean external impediments of motion; and may be applied no less to irrational, and inanimate creatures, than to rational. For whatsoever is so tied, or environed, as it cannot move but within a certain space, which space is determined by the opposition of some external body, we say it hath not liberty to go further. And so of all living creatures, whilst they are imprisoned, or restrained, with walls, or chains; and of the water whilst it is kept in by banks, or vessels, that otherwise would spread itself into a larger space, we use to say, they are not at liberty, to move in such manner, as without those external imped-

iments they would. But when the impediment of
motion, is in the constitution of the thing itself, we use
not to say; it wants the liberty; but the power to move;
as when a stone lieth still, or a man is fastened to his
bed by sickness.

What it is to be free.

And according to this proper, and generally received
meaning of the word, a freeman, is he, that in those
things, which by his strength and wit he is able to do,
is not hindered to do what he has a will to. But when
the words free, and liberty, are applied to any thing
but bodies, they are abused; for that which is not subject to motion, is not subject to impediment: and
therefore, when it is said, for example, the way is free,
no liberty of the way is signified, but of those that
walk in it without stop. And when we say a gift is free,
there is not meant any liberty of the gift, but of the
giver, that was not bound by any law or covenant to
give it. So when we speak freely, it is not the liberty of
voice, or pronunciation, but of the man, whom no law
hath obliged to speak otherwise than he did. Lastly,
from the use of the word free-will, no liberty can be
inferred of the will, desire, or inclination, but the liberty of the man; which consisteth in this, that he finds
no stop, in doing what he has the will, desire, or inclination to do.

Fear and liberty are consistent.

Fear and liberty are consistent; as when a man throweth his goods into the sea for fear the ship should sink, he doth it nevertheless very willingly, and may refuse to do it if he will: it is therefore the action of one that was free: so a man sometimes pays his debt, only for fear of imprisonment, which because nobody hindered him from detaining, was the action of a man at liberty. And generally all actions which men do in commonwealths, for fear of the law, are actions, which the doers had liberty to omit.

Liberty and necessity consistent.

Liberty, and necessity are consistent: as in the water, that hath not only liberty, but a necessity of descending by the channel; so likewise in the actions which men voluntarily do: which, because they proceed from their will, proceed from liberty; and yet, because every act of man's will, and every desire, and inclination proceedeth from some cause, and that from another cause, in a continual chain, whose first link is in the hand of God the first of all causes, proceed from necessity. So that to him that could see the connexion of those causes, the necessity of all men's voluntary actions, would appear manifest. And therefore God, that seeth, and disposeth all things, seeth also that the liberty of man in doing what he will, is accompanied with the necessity of doing that which God will, and no more, nor less. For though men may do many things, which God does not command, nor is therefore author of them; yet they can have no passion, nor appetite to anything, of which appetite God's will is not the cause. And did not his will assure the necessity of man's will, and consequently of all that on man's will dependeth, the liberty of men would be a contradiction, and impediment to the omnipotence and liberty of God. And this shall suffice, as to the matter in hand, of that natural liberty, which only is properly called liberty.

ARTIFICIAL BONDS, OR COVENANTS.

But as men, for the attaining of peace, and conservation of themselves thereby, have made an artificial man, which we call a commonwealth; so also have they made artificial chains, called civil laws, which they themselves, by mutual covenants, have fastened at one end, to the lips of that man, or assembly, to whom they have given the sovereign power; and at the other end to their own ears. These bonds, in their own nature but weak, may nevertheless be made to hold, by the danger, though not by the difficulty of breaking them.

LIBERTY OF SUBJECTS CONSISTETH
IN LIBERTY FROM COVENANTS.

In relation to these bonds only it is, that I am to speak now, of the liberty of subjects. For seeing there is no commonwealth in the world, wherein there be rules enough set down, for the regulating of all the actions, and words of men; as being a thing impossible: it followeth necessarily, that in all kinds of actions by the laws prætermitted, men have the liberty, of doing what their own reasons shall suggest, for the most profitable to themselves. For if we take liberty in the proper sense, for corporal liberty; that is to say, freedom from chains and prison; it were very absurd for men to clamour as they do, for the liberty they so manifestly enjoy. Again, if we take liberty, for an exemption from laws, it is it no less absurd, for men to demand as they do, that liberty, by which all other men may be masters of their lives. And yet, as absurd as it is, this is it they demand; not knowing that the laws are of no power to protect them, without a sword in the hands of a man, or men, to cause those laws to be put in execution. The liberty of a subject, lieth therefore only in those things, which in regulating their actions, the sovereign hath prætermitted: such as is the liberty to buy, and sell, and otherwise contract with one another; to choose their own abode, their own diet, their own trade of life, and institute their children as they themselves think fit; and the like.

Liberty of the subject consistent with the unlimited power of the sovereign.

Nevertheless we are not to understand, that by such liberty, the sovereign power of life and death, is either abolished, or limited. For it has been already shown, that nothing the sovereign representative can do to a subject, on what pretence soever, can properly be called injustice, or injury; because every subject is author of every act the sovereign doth; so that he never wanteth right to anything, otherwise, than as he himself is the subject of God, and bound thereby to observe the laws of nature. And therefore it may, and doth often happen in commonwealths, that a subject may be put to death, by the command of the sovereign power; and yet neither do the other wrong: as when Jephtha caused his daughter to be sacrificed: in which, and the like cases, he that so dieth, had liberty to do the action, for which he is nevertheless, without injury put to death. And the same holdeth also in a sovereign prince, that putteth to death an innocent subject. For though the action be against the law of nature, as being contrary to equity, as was the killing of Uriah, by David; yet it was not an injury to Uriah, but to God. Not to Uriah, because the right to do what he pleased was given him by Uriah himself: and yet to God, because David was God's subject, and prohibited all iniquity by the law of nature: which distinction, David himself, when he repented the fact, evidently confirmed, saying, To thee only have I sinned. In the same manner, the people of Athens, when they banished the most potent of their commonwealth for ten years, thought they committed no injustice; and yet they never questioned what crime he had done; but what hurt he would do: nay they commanded the banishment of they knew not whom; and every citizen bringing his oystershell into the market place, written with the name of him he desired should be banished, without actually accusing him, sometimes banished an Aristides, for his reputation of justice; and sometimes a scurrilous jester, as Hyperbolus, to make a jest of it. And yet a man cannot say, the sovereign people of Athens wanted right to banish them; or an Athenian the liberty to jest, or to be just.

THE LIBERTY WHICH WRITERS PRAISE, IS THE LIBERTY OF SOVEREIGNS; NOT OF PRIVATE MEN.

The liberty, whereof there is so frequent and honourable mention, in the histories, and philosophy of the ancient Greeks, and Romans, and in the writings, and discourse of those that from them have received all their learning in the politics, is not the liberty of particular men; but the liberty of the commonwealth: which is the same with that which every man then should have, if there were no civil laws, nor commonwealth at all. And the effects of it also be the same. For as amongst masterless men, there is perpetual war, of every man against his neighbour; no inheritance, to transmit to the son, nor to expect from the father; no propriety of goods, or lands; no security; but a full and absolute liberty in every particular man: so in states, and commonwealths not dependent on one another, every commonwealth, not every man, has an absolute liberty, to do what it shall judge, that is to say, what that man, or assembly that representeth it, shall judge most conducing to their benefit. But withal, they live in the condition of a perpetual war, and upon the confines of battle, with their frontiers armed, and cannons planted against their neighbours round about. The Athenians, and Romans were free; that is, free commonwealths: not that any particular men had the liberty to resist their own representative; but that their representative had the liberty to resist, or invade other people. There is written on the turrets of the city of Lucca in great characters at this day, the word libertas; yet no man can thence infer, that a particular man has more liberty, or immunity from the service of the commonwealth there, than in Constantinople. Whether a commonwealth be monarchical, or popular, the freedom is still the same.

But it is an easy thing, for men to be deceived, by the specious name of liberty; and for want of judgment to distinguish, mistake that for their private inheritance, and birth-right, which is the right of the public only. And when the same error is confirmed by the authority of men in reputation for their writings on this subject, it is no wonder if it produce sedition, and change of government. In these western parts of

the world, we are made to receive our opinions concerning the institution, and rights of commonwealths, from
Aristotle, Cicero, and other men, Greeks and Romans,
that living under popular states, derived those rights, not
from the principles of nature, but transcribed them into
their books, out of the practice of their own commonwealths, which were popular; as the grammarians
describe the rules of language, out of the practice of
the time; or the rules of poetry, out of the poems of Homer
and Virgil. And because the Athenians were taught, to
keep them from desire of changing their government,
that they were freemen, and all that lived under monarchy were slaves; therefore Aristotle puts it down in
his Politics, (lib. 6. cap. ii.) In democracy, liberty is to
be supposed: for it is commonly held, that no man is
free in any other government. And as Aristotle; so
Cicero, and other writers have grounded their civil
doctrine, on the opinions of the Romans, who were
taught to hate monarchy, at first, by them that having
deposed their sovereign, shared amongst them the sovereignty of Rome; and afterwards by their successors.
And by reading of these Greek, and Latin authors,
men from their childhood have gotten a habit, under a
false show of liberty, of favouring tumults, and of
licentious controlling the actions of their sovereigns,
and again of controlling those controllers; with the
effusion of so much blood, as I think I may truly say,

there was never any thing so dearly bought, as these western parts have bought the learning of the Greek and Latin tongues.

LIBERTY OF SUBJECTS HOW TO BE MEASURED.

To come now to the particulars of the true liberty of a subject; that is to say, what are the things, which though commanded by the sovereign, he may nevertheless, without injustice, refuse to do; we are to consider, what rights we pass away, when we make a commonwealth; or, which is all one, what liberty we deny ourselves, by owning all the actions, without exception, of the man, or assembly we make our sovereign. For in the act of our submission, consisteth both our obligation, and our liberty; which must therefore be inferred by arguments taken from thence; there being no obligation on any man, which ariseth not from some act of his own; for all men equally, are by nature free. And because such arguments, must either be drawn from the express words, I authorize all his actions, or from the intention of him that submitteth himself to his power, which intention is to be understood by the end for which he so submitteth; the obligation, and liberty of the subject, is to be derived, either from those words, or others equivalent; or else from the end of the institution of sovereignty, namely, the peace of the subjects within themselves, and their defence against a common enemy.

SUBJECTS HAVE LIBERTY TO DEFEND THEIR OWN BODIES, EVEN AGAINST THEM THAT LAWFULLY INVADE THEM.

First therefore, seeing sovereignty by institution, is by covenant of every one to every one; and sovereignty by acquisition, by covenants of the vanquished to the victor, or child to the parent; it is manifest, that every subject has liberty in all those things, the right whereof cannot by covenant be transferred. I have shewn before in the 14th chapter, that covenants, not to defend a man's own body, are void. Therefore,

ARE NOT BOUND TO HURT THEMSELVES.

If the sovereign command a man, though justly condemned, to kill, wound, or maim himself; or not to resist those that assault him; or to abstain from the use of food, air, medicine, or any other thing, without which he cannot live; yet hath that man the liberty to disobey.

If a man be interrogated by the sovereign, or his authority, concerning a crime done by himself, he is not bound, without assurance of pardon, to confess it; because no man, as I have shown in the same chapter, can be obliged by covenant to accuse himself.

Again, the consent of a subject to sovereign power, is contained in these words, I authorize, or take upon me, all his actions; in which there is no restriction at all, of his own former natural liberty: for by allowing him to kill me, I am not bound to kill myself when he commands me. It is one thing to say, kill me, or my fellow, if you please; another thing to say, I will kill myself, or my fellow. It followeth therefore, that

No man is bound by the words themselves, either to kill himself, or any other man; and consequently, that the obligation a man may sometimes have, upon the command of the sovereign to execute any dangerous, or dishonourable office, dependeth not on the words of our submission; but on the intention, which is to be understood by the end thereof. When therefore our refusal to obey, frustrates the end for which the sovereignty was ordained; then there is no liberty to refuse: otherwise there is.

NOR TO WARFARE, UNLESS THEY VOLUNTARILY UNDERTAKE IT. Upon this ground, a man that is commanded as a soldier to fight against the enemy, though his sovereign have right enough to punish his refusal with death, may nevertheless in many cases refuse, without injustice; as when he substituteth a sufficient soldier in his place: for in this case he deserteth not the service of the commonwealth. And there is allowance to be made for natural timorousness; not only to women, of whom no such dangerous duty is expected, but also to men of feminine courage. When armies fight, there is on one side, or both, a running away; yet when they do it not out of treachery, but fear, they are not esteemed to do it unjustly, but dishonourably. For the same reason, to avoid battle, is not injustice, but cowardice. But he that inrolleth himself a soldier, or taketh imprest money, taketh away the excuse of a timorous nature; and is obliged, not only to go to the battle, but also not to run from it, without his captain's leave. And when the defence of the commonwealth, requireth at once the help of all that are able to bear arms, every one is obliged; because otherwise the institution of the commonwealth, which they have not the purpose, or courage to preserve, was in vain.

To resist the sword of the commonwealth, in defence of another man, guilty, or innocent, no man hath liberty; because such liberty, takes away from the sovereign, the means of protecting us; and is therefore destructive of the very essence of government. But in case a great many men together, have already resisted the sovereign power unjustly, or committed some capital crime, for which every one of them expecteth death, whether have they not the liberty then to join together, and assist, and defend one another? Certainly they have: for they but defend their lives, which the guilty man may as well do, as the innocent. There was indeed injustice in the first breach of their duty; their bearing of arms subsequent to it, though it be to maintain what they have done, is no new unjust act. And if it be only to defend their persons, it is not unjust at all. But the offer of pardon taketh from them, to whom it is offered, the plea of self-defence, and maketh their perseverance in assisting, or defending the rest, unlawful.

THE GREATEST LIBERTY OF SUBJECTS,
DEPENDETH ON THE SILENCE OF THE LAW.

As for other liberties, they depend on the silence of the law. In cases where the sovereign has prescribed no rule, there the subject hath the liberty to do, or forbear, according to his own discretion. And therefore such liberty is in some places more, and in some less; and in some times more, in other times less, according as they that have the sovereignty shall think most convenient. As for example, there was a time, when in England a man might enter into his own land, and dispossess such as wrongfully possessed it, by force. But in aftertimes, that liberty of forcible entry, was taken away by a statute made, by the king, in parliament. And in some places of the world, men have the liberty of many wives: in other places, such liberty is not allowed.

If a subject have a controversy with his sovereign, of debt, or of right of possession of lands or goods, or concerning any service required at his hands, or concerning any penalty, corporal, or pecuniary, grounded on a precedent law; he hath the same liberty to sue for his right, as if it were against a subject; and before such judges, as are appointed by the sovereign. For seeing the sovereign demandeth by force of a former law, and not by virtue of his power; he declareth thereby, that he requireth no more, than shall appear to be due by that law. The suit therefore is not contrary to the will of the sovereign; and consequently the subject hath the liberty to demand the hearing of his cause; and sentence, according to that law. But if he demand, or take anything by pretence of his power; there lieth, in that case, no action of law; for all that is done by him in virtue of his power, is done by the authority of every subject, and consequently he that brings an action against the sovereign, brings it against himself.

If a monarch, or sovereign assembly, grant a liberty to all, or any of his subjects, which grant standing, he is disabled to provide for their safety, the grant is void; unless he directly renounce, or transfer the sovereignty to another. For in that he might openly, if it had been his will, and in plain terms, have renounced, or transferred it, and did not; it is to be understood it was not his will, but that the grant proceeded from ignorance of the repugnancy between such a liberty and the sovereign power; and therefore the sovereignty is still retained; and consequently all those powers, which are necessary to the exercising thereof; such as are the power of war, and peace, of judicature, of appointing officers, and councillors, of levying money, and the rest named in the 18th chapter.

In what cases subjects are absolved
of their obedience to their sovereign.

The obligation of subjects to the sovereign, is understood to last as long, and no longer, than the power lasteth, by which he is able to protect them. For the right men have by nature to protect themselves, when none else can protect them, can by no covenant be relinquished. The sovereignty is the soul of the commonwealth; which once departed from the body, the members do no more receive their motion from it. The end of obedience is protection; which, wheresoever a man seeth it, either in his own, or in another's sword, nature applieth his obedience to it, and his endeavour to maintain it. And though sovereignty, in the intention of them that make it, be immortal; yet is it in its own nature, not only subject to violent death, by foreign war; but also through the ignorance, and passions of men, it hath in it, from the very institution, many seeds of a natural mortality, by intestine discord.

In case of captivity.

If a subject be taken prisoner in war; or his person, or his means of life be within the guards of the enemy, and hath his life and corporal liberty given him, on condition to be subject to the victor, he hath liberty to accept the condition; and having accepted it, is the subject of him that took him; because he had no other way to preserve himself. The case is the same, if he be detained on the same terms, in a foreign country. But if a man be held in prison, or bonds, or is not trusted with the liberty of his body; he cannot be understood to be bound by covenant to subjection; and therefore may, if he can, make his escape by any means whatsoever.

In case the sovereign cast off the government from himself and his heirs.

If a monarch shall relinquish the sovereignty, both for himself, and his heirs; his subjects return to the absolute liberty of nature; because, though nature may declare who are his sons, and who are the nearest of his kin; yet it dependeth on his own will, as hath been said in the precedent chapter, who shall be his heir. If therefore he will have no heir, there is no sovereignty, nor subjection. The case is the same, if he die without known kindred, and without declaration of his heir. For then there can no heir be known, and consequently no subjection be due.

In case of banishment.

If the sovereign banish his subject; during the banishment, he is not subject. But he that is sent on a message, or hath leave to travel, is still subject; but it is, by contract between sovereigns, not by virtue of the covenant of subjection. For whosoever entereth into another's dominion, is subject to all the laws thereof; unless he have a privilege by the amity of the sovereigns, or by special licence.

In case the sovereign render himself subject to another.

If a monarch subdued by war, render himself subject to the victor; his subjects are delivered from their former obligation, and become obliged to the victor. But if he be held prisoner, or have not the liberty of his own body; he is not understood to have given away the right of sovereignty; and therefore his subjects are obliged to yield obedience to the magistrates formerly placed, governing not in their own name, but in his. For, his right remaining, the question is only of the administration; that is to say, of the magistrates and officers; which, if he have not means to name, he is supposed to approve those, which he himself had formerly appointed.

CHAPTER XXXI

OF THE KINGDOM OF GOD BY NATURE

The scope of the following chapters.

That the condition of mere nature, that is to say, of absolute liberty, such as is theirs, that neither are sovereigns, nor subjects, is anarchy, and the condition of war: that the precepts, by which men are guided to avoid that condition, are the laws of nature: that a commonwealth, without sovereign power, is but a word without substance, and cannot stand: that subjects owe to sovereigns, simple obedience, in all things wherein their obedience is not repugnant to the laws of God, I have sufficiently proved, in that which I have already written. There wants only, for the entire knowledge of civil duty, to know what are those laws of God. For without that, a man knows not, when he is commanded any thing by the civil power, whether it be contrary to the law of God, or not: and so, either by too much civil obedience, offends the Divine Majesty; or through fear of offending God, transgresses the commandments of the commonwealth. To avoid both these rocks, it is necessary to know what are the laws divine. And seeing the knowledge of all law, dependeth on the knowledge of the sovereign power, I shall say something in that which followeth, of the Kingdom of God.

WHO ARE SUBJECTS IN THE KINGDOM OF GOD.

God is king, let the earth rejoice, saith the psalmist. (xcvii. 1). And again, (Psalm xcix. 1) God is king, though the nations be angry; and he that sitteth on the cherubims, though the earth be moved. Whether men will or not, they must be subject always to the divine power. By denying the existence, or providence of God, men may shake off their ease, but not their yoke. But to call this power of God, which extendeth itself not only

to man, but also to beasts, and plants, and bodies inanimate, by the name of kingdom, is but a metaphorical
use of the word. For he only is properly said to reign,
that governs his subjects by his word, and by promise of
rewards to those that obey it, and by threatening them
with punishment that obey it not. Subjects therefore in
the kingdom of God, are not bodies inanimate, nor
creatures irrational; because they understand no precepts as his: nor atheists, nor they that believe not that
God has any care of the actions of mankind; because
they acknowledge no word for his, nor have hope of his
rewards or fear of his threatenings. They therefore that
believe there is a God that governeth the world, and
hath given precepts, and propounded rewards, and punishments to mankind, are God's subjects; all the rest,
are to be understood as enemies.

A THREEFOLD WORD OF GOD,
REASON, REVELATION, PROPHECY.

To rule by words, requires that such words be manifestly
made known; for else they are no laws: for to the nature of
laws belongeth a sufficient, and clear promulgation, such
as may take away the excuse of ignorance; which in the
laws of men is but of one only kind, and that is, proclama-
tion, or promulgation by the voice of man. But God
declareth his laws three ways; by the dictates of natural
reason, by revelation, and by the voice of some man, to

whom by the operation of miracles, he procureth credit with the rest. From hence there ariseth a triple word of God, rational, sensible, and prophetic: to which correspondeth a triple hearing; right reason, sense supernatural, and faith. As for sense supernatural, which consisteth in revelation or inspiration, there have not been any universal laws so given, because God speaketh not in that manner but to particular persons, and to divers men divers things.

A TWOFOLD KINGDOM OF GOD, NATURAL AND PROPHETIC.

From the difference between the other two kinds of God's word, rational, and prophetic, there may be attributed to God, a twofold kingdom, natural, and prophetic: natural, wherein he governeth as many of mankind as acknowledge his providence, by the natural dictates of right reason; and prophetic, wherein having chosen out one peculiar nation, the Jews, for his subjects, he governed them, and none but them, not only by natural reason, but by positive laws, which he gave them by the mouths of his holy prophets. Of the natural kingdom of God I intend to speak in this chapter.

THE RIGHT OF GOD'S SOVEREIGNTY IS DERIVED FROM HIS OMNIPOTENCE.

The right of nature, whereby God reigneth over men, and punisheth those that break his laws, is to be derived, not from his creating them, as if he required obedience as of gratitude for his benefits; but from his irresistible power. I have formerly shown, how the sovereign right ariseth from pact: to show how the same right may arise from nature, requires no more, but to show in what case it is never taken away. Seeing all men by nature had right to all things, they had right every one to reign over all the rest. But because this right could not be obtained by force, it concerned the safety of every one, laying by that right, to set up men, with sovereign authority, by common consent, to rule and defend them: whereas if there had been any man of power irresistible, there had been no reason, why he should not by that power have ruled and defended both himself, and them, according to his own discretion. To those therefore whose power is irresistible, the dominion of all men adhereth naturally by their excellence of power; and consequently it is from that power, that the kingdom over men, and the right of afflicting men at his pleasure, belongeth naturally to God Almighty; not as Creator, and gracious; but as omnipotent. And though punishment be due for sin only, because by that word is understood affliction for sin; yet the right of afflicting, is not always derived from men's sin, but from God's power.

Sin not the cause of all affliction.

This question, why evil men often prosper, and good men suffer adversity, has been much disputed by the

ancient, and is the same with this of ours, by what right
God dispenseth the prosperities and adversities of this
life; and is of that difficulty, as it hath shaken the faith,
not only of the vulgar, but of philosophers, and which
is more, of the Saints, concerning the Divine Providence. How good, saith David, (Psalm lxxiii. I, 2, 3) is
the God of Israel to those that are upright in heart; and
yet my feet were almost gone, my treadings had well-
nigh slipt; for I was grieved at the wicked, when I saw
the ungodly in such prosperity. And Job, how earnestly
does he expostulate with God, for the many afflictions
he suffered, notwithstanding his righteousness? This
question in the case of Job, is decided by God himself,
not by arguments derived from Job's sin, but his own
power. For whereas the friends of Job drew their arguments from his affliction to his sin, and he defended
himself by the conscience of his innocence, God himself taketh up the matter, and having justified the affliction by arguments drawn from his power, such as this,
(Job xxxviii. 4) Where wast thou, when I laid the foun-
dations of the earth? and the like, both approved Job's
innocence, and reproved the erroneous doctrine of his
friends. Conformable to this doctrine is the sentence of
our Saviour, concerning the man that was born blind, in
these words, Neither hath this man sinned, nor his
fathers; but that the works of God might be made manifest in him. And though it be said, that death entered

into the world by sin, (by which is meant, that if Adam had never sinned, he had never died, that is, never suffered any separation of his soul from his body), it follows not thence, that God could not justly have afflicted him, though he had not sinned, as well as he afflicteth other living creatures, that cannot sin.

DIVINE LAWS.

Having spoken of the right of God's sovereignty, as grounded only on nature; we are to consider next, what are the Divine laws, or dictates of natural reason; which laws concern either the natural duties of one man to another, or the honour naturally due to our Divine Sovereign. The first are the same laws of nature, of which I have spoken already in the fourteenth and fifteenth chapters of this treatise; namely, equity, justice, mercy, humility, and the rest of the moral virtues. It remaineth therefore that we consider, what precepts are dictated to men, by their natural reason only, without other word of God, touching the honour and worship of the Divine Majesty.

HONOUR AND WORSHIP, WHAT.

Honour consisteth in the inward thought, and opinion of the power, and goodness of another; and therefore to honour God, is to think as highly of his power and goodness, as is possible. And of that opinion, the external signs appearing in the words and actions of men, are called worship; which is one part of that which the Latins understand by the word *cultus*. For *cultus* signifieth properly, and constantly, that labour which a man bestows on anything, with a purpose to make benefit by it. Now those things whereof we make benefit, are either subject to us, and the profit they yield, followeth the labour we bestow upon them, as a natural effect; or they are not subject to us, but answer our labour, according to their own wills. In the first sense the labour bestowed on the earth, is called culture; and the education of children, a culture of their minds. In the second sense, where men's wills are to be wrought to our purpose, not by force, but by complaisance, it signifieth as much as courting, that is, a winning of favour by good offices; as by praises, by acknowledging their power, and by whatsoever is pleasing to them from whom we look for any benefit. And this is properly worship: in which sense Publicola, is understood for a worshipper of the people; and *cultus Dei*, for the worship of God.

Several signs of honour.

From internal honour, consisting in the opinion of power and goodness, arise three passions; love, which hath reference to goodness; and hope, and fear, that relate to power: and three parts of external worship; praise, magnifying, and blessing: the subject of praise, being goodness; the subject of magnifying and blessing, being power, and the effect thereof felicity. Praise, and magnifying are signified both by words, and actions: by words, when we say a man is good, or great: by actions, when we thank him for his bounty, and obey his power. The opinion of the happiness of another, can only be expressed by words.

Worship natural and arbitrary.

There be some signs of honour, both in attributes and actions, that be naturally so; as amongst attributes, good, just, liberal, and the like; and amongst actions, prayers, thanks, and obedience. Others are so by institution, or custom of men; and in some times and places are honourable; in others, dishonourable; in others, indifferent: such as are the gestures in salutation, prayer, and thanksgiving, in different times and places, differently used. The former is natural; the latter arbitrary worship.

Worship commanded and free.

And of arbitrary worship, there be two differences: for sometimes it is a commanded, sometimes voluntary worship: commanded, when it is such as he requireth, who is worshipped: free, when it is such as the worshipper thinks fit. When it is commanded, not the words, or gesture, but the obedience is the worship. But when

free, the worship consists in the opinion of the behold-
ers: for if to them the words, or actions by which we
intend honour, seem ridiculous, and tending to contumely, they are no worship, because no signs of honour;
and no signs of honour, because a sign is not a sign to
him that giveth it, but to him to whom it is made, that
is, to the spectator.

Worship public and private.

Again, there is a public, and a private worship. Public, is
the worship that a commonwealth performeth, as one
person. Private, is that which a private person exhib-
iteth. Public, in respect of the whole commonwealth, is
free; but in respect of particular men, it is not so. Private, is in secret free; but in the sight of the multitude,
it is never without some restraint, either from the laws,
or from the opinion of men; which is contrary to the
nature of liberty.

The end of worship.

The end of worship amongst men, is power. For
where a man seeth another worshipped, he supposeth
him powerful, and is the readier to obey him; which
makes his power greater. But God has no ends: the
worship we do him, proceeds from our duty, and is
directed according to our capacity, by those rules of
honour, that reason dictateth to be done by the weak

to the more potent men, in hope of benefit, for fear of damage, or in thankfulness for good already received from them.

ATTRIBUTES OF DIVINE HONOUR.

That we may know what worship of God is taught us by the light of nature, I will begin with his attributes. Where, first, it is manifest, we ought to attribute to him existence. For no man can have the will to honour that, which he thinks not to have any being.

Secondly, that those philosophers, who said the world, or the soul of the world was God, spake unworthily of him; and denied his existence. For by God, is understood the cause of the world; and to say the world is God, is to say there is no cause of it, that is, no God.

Thirdly, to say the world was not created, but eternal, seeing that which is eternal has no cause, is to deny there is a God.

Fourthly, that they who attributing, as they think, ease to God, take from him the care of mankind; take from him his honour: for it takes away men's love, and fear of him; which is the root of honour.

Fifthly, in those things that signify greatness, and power; to say he is finite, is not to honour him: for it is not a sign of the will to honour God, to attribute to him less than we can; and finite, is less than we can; because to finite, it is easy to add more.

Therefore to attribute figure to him, is not honour; for all figure is finite:

Nor to say we conceive, and imagine, or have an idea of him, in our mind: for whatsoever we conceive is finite:

Nor to attribute to him parts, or totality; which are the attributes only of things finite:

Nor to say he is in this, or that place: for whatsoever is in place, is bounded, and finite:

Nor that he is moved, or resteth: for both these attributes ascribe to him place:

Nor that there be more Gods than one; because it implies them all finite: for there cannot be more than one infinite:

Nor to ascribe to him, (unless metaphorically, meaning not the passion but the effect), passions that partake of grief; as repentance, anger, mercy: or of want; as appetite, hope, desire; or of any passive faculty: for passion, is power limited by somewhat else.

And therefore when we ascribe to God a will, it is not to be understood, as that of man, for a rational appetite; but as the power, by which he effecteth every thing.

Likewise when we attribute to him sight, and other acts of sense; as also knowledge, and understanding; which in us is nothing else, but a tumult of the mind, raised by external things that press the organical parts of man's body: for there is no such thing in God; and being things that depend on natural causes, cannot be attributed to him.

He that will attribute to God, nothing but what is warranted by natural reason, must either use such negative attributes, as infinite, eternal, incomprehensible; or superlatives, as most high, most great, and the like; or indefinite, as good, just, holy, creator; and in such sense, as if he meant not to declare what he is, (for that were to circumscribe him within the limits of our fancy), but how much we admire him, and how ready we would be to obey him; which is a sign of humility, and of a will to honour him as much as we can. For there is but one name to signify our conception of his nature, and that is, I am: and but one name of his relation to us, and that is, God; in which is contained Father, King, and Lord.

ACTIONS THAT ARE SIGNS OF DIVINE HONOUR.

Concerning the actions of divine worship, it is a most general precept of reason, that they be signs of the intention to honour God; such as are, first, prayers. For not the carvers, when they made images, were thought to make them gods; but the people that prayed to them.

Secondly, thanksgiving; which differeth from prayer in divine worship, no otherwise, than that prayers precede, and thanks succeed the benefit; the end, both of the one and the other, being to acknowledge God, for author of all benefits, as well past, as future.

Thirdly, gifts, that is to say, sacrifices and oblations, if they be of the best, are signs of honour: for they are thanksgivings.

Fourthly, not to swear by any but God, is naturally a sign of honour: for it is a confession that God only knoweth the heart; and that no man's wit or strength can protect a man against God's vengeance on the perjured.

Fifthly, it is a part of rational worship, to speak considerately of God; for it argues a fear of him, and fear is a confession of his power. Hence followeth, that the name of God is not to be used rashly, and to no purpose; for that is as much, as in vain: and it is to no purpose, unless it be by way of oath, and by order of the commonwealth, to make judgments certain; or between commonwealths, to avoid war. And that disputing of God's nature is contrary to his honour: for it is supposed, that in this natural kingdom of God, there is no other way to know anything, but by natural reason, that is, from the principles of natural science; which are so far from teaching us any thing of God's nature, as they cannot teach us our own nature, nor the nature of the smallest creature living. And therefore, when men out of the principles of natural reason, dispute of the attributes of God, they but dishonour him: for in the attributes which we give to God, we are not to consider the signification of philosophical truth; but the signification of pious intention, to do him the greatest honour we are able. From the want of which consideration, have proceeded the volumes of disputation about the nature of God, that tend not to his honour, but to the honour of our own wits and learning; and are nothing else but inconsiderate and vain abuses of his sacred name.

Sixthly, in prayers, thanksgivings, offerings, and sacrifices, it is a dictate of natural reason, that they be every one in his kind the best, and most significant of honour. As for example, that prayers and thanksgiving, be made in words and phrases, not sudden, nor light, nor plebeian; but beautiful, and well composed. For else we do not God as much honour as we can. And therefore the heathens did absurdly, to worship images for gods: but their doing it in verse, and with music, both of voice and instruments, was reasonable. Also that the beasts they offered in sacrifice, and the gifts they offered, and their actions in worshipping, were full of submission, and commemorative of benefits received, was according to reason, as proceeding from an intention to honour him.

Seventhly, reason directeth not only to worship God in secret; but also, and especially, in public, and in the sight of men. For without that, that which in honour is most acceptable, the procuring others to honour him, is lost.

Lastly, obedience to his laws, that is, in this case to the laws of nature, is the greatest worship of all. For as obedience is more acceptable to God than sacrifice; so also to set light by his commandments, is the greatest of all contumelies. And these are the laws of that divine worship, which natural reason dictateth to private men.

PUBLIC WORSHIP CONSISTETH IN UNIFORMITY.

But seeing a commonwealth is but one person, it ought also to exhibit to God but one worship; which then it doth, when it commandeth it to be exhibited by private men, publicly. And this is public worship; the property whereof, is to be uniform: for those actions that are done differently, by different men, cannot be said to be a public worship. And therefore, where many sorts of worship be allowed, proceeding from the different religions of private men, it cannot be said there is any public worship, nor that the commonwealth is of any religion at all.

ALL ATTRIBUTES DEPEND ON THE LAWS CIVIL.

And because words, and consequently the attributes of God, have their signification by agreement and constitution of men, those attributes are to be held significative of honour, that men intend shall so be; and whatsoever may be done by the wills of particular men, where there is no law but reason, may be done by the will of the commonwealth, by laws civil. And because a commonwealth hath no will, nor makes no laws, but those that are made by the will of him, or them that have the sovereign power; it followeth that those attributes which the sovereign ordaineth, in the worship of God, for signs of honour, ought to be taken and used for such, by private men in their public worship.

Not all actions.

But because not all actions are signs by constitution, but some are naturally signs of honour, others of contumely; these latter, which are those that men are ashamed to do in the sight of them they reverence, cannot be made by human power a part of Divine worship; nor the former, such as are decent, modest, humble behaviour, ever be separated from it. But whereas there be an infinite number of actions and gestures of an indifferent nature; such of them as the commonwealth shall ordain to be publicly and universally in use, as signs of honour, and part of God's worship, are to be taken and used for such by the subjects. And that which is said in the Scripture, It is better to obey God than man, hath place in the kingdom of God by pact, and not by nature.

Natural punishments.

Having thus briefly spoken of the natural kingdom of God, and his natural laws, I will add only to this chapter a short declaration of his natural punishments. There is no action of man in this life, that is not the beginning of so long a chain of consequences, as no human providence is high enough, to give a man a prospect to the end. And in this chain, there are linked together both pleasing and unpleasing events; in such manner, as he that will do anything for his pleasure, must engage himself to suffer all the pains annexed to it; and these pains, are the natural punishments of those actions, which are the beginning of more harm than good. And hereby it comes to pass, that intemperance is naturally punished with diseases; rashness, with mischances; injustice, with the violence of enemies; pride, with ruin; cowardice, with oppression: negligent government of princes, with rebellion; and rebellion, with slaughter. For seeing punishments are consequent to the breach of laws; natural punishments must be naturally consequent to the breach of the laws of nature; and therefore follow them as their natural, not arbitrary effects.

THE CONCLUSION OF THE SECOND PART. CONCLUSION.

And thus far concerning the constitution, nature, and right of sovereigns, and concerning the duty of subjects, derived from the principles of natural reason. And now, considering how different this doctrine is, from the practice of the greatest part of the world, especially of these western parts, that have received their moral learning from Rome and Athens; and how much depth of moral philosophy is required, in them that have the administration of the sovereign power; I am at the point of believing this my labour, as useless, as the commonwealth of Plato. For he also is of opinion that it is impossible for the disorders of state, and change of governments by civil war, ever to be taken away, till sovereigns be philosophers. But when I consider again, that the science of natural justice, is the only science necessary for sovereigns and their principal ministers; and that they need not be charged with the sciences mathematical, as by Plato they are, farther than by good laws to encourage men to the study of them; and that neither Plato, nor any other philosopher hitherto, hath put into order, and sufficiently or probably proved all the theorems of moral doctrine, that men may learn thereby, both how to govern, and how to obey; I recover some hope, that one time or other, this writing of mine may fall into the hands of a sovereign, who will consider it himself, (for it is short, and I think clear), without the help of any interested, or envious interpreter; and by the exercise of entire sovereignty, in protecting the public teaching of it, convert this truth of speculation, into the utility of practice.

Chapter XLVII

. . .

COMPARISON OF THE PAPACY WITH THE KINGDOM OF FAIRIES. But after this doctrine, that the Church now militant, is the kingdom of God spoken of in the Old and New Testament, was received in the world; the ambition, and canvassing for the offices that belong thereunto, and especially for that great office of being Christ's lieutenant, and the pomp of them that obtained therein the principal public charges, became by degrees so evident, that they lost the inward reverence due to the pastoral function: insomuch as the wisest men, of them that had any power in the civil state, needed nothing but the authority of their princes, to deny them any further obedience. For, from the time that the Bishop of Rome had gotten to be acknowledged for bishop universal, by pretence of succession to St. Peter, their whole hierarchy, or kingdom of darkness, may be compared not unfitly to the kingdom of fairies; that is, to the old wives' fables in England, concerning ghosts and spirits, and the feats they play in the night. And if a man consider the original of this great ecclesiastical dominion, he will easily perceive, that the Papacy is no other than the ghost of the deceased

Roman empire, sitting crowned upon the grave thereof. For so did the Papacy start up on a sudden out of the ruins of that heathen power.

The language also, which they use, both in the churches, and in their public acts, being Latin, which is not commonly used by any nation now in the world, what is it but the ghost of the old Roman language?

The fairies in what nation soever they converse, have but one universal king, which some poets of ours call King Oberon; but the Scripture calls Beelzebub, prince of demons. The ecclesiastics likewise, in whose dominions soever they be found, acknowledge but one universal king, the Pope.

The ecclesiastics are spiritual men, and ghostly fathers. The fairies are spirits, and ghosts. Fairies and ghosts inhabit darkness, solitudes, and graves. The ecclesiastics walk in obscurity of doctrine, in monasteries, churches, and church-yards.

The ecclesiastics have their cathedral churches, which, in what town soever they be erected, by virtue of holy water, and certain charms called exorcisms, have the power to make those towns, cities, that is to say, seats of empire. The fairies also have their enchanted castles, and certain gigantic ghosts, that domineer over the regions round about them.

The fairies are not to be seized on; and brought to

answer for the hurt they do. So also the ecclesiastics vanish away from the tribunals of civil justice.

The ecclesiastics take from young men the use of reason, by certain charms compounded of metaphysics, and miracles, and traditions, and abused Scripture, whereby they are good for nothing else, but to execute what they command them. The fairies likewise are said to take young children out of their cradles, and to change them into natural fools, which common people do therefore call elves, and are apt to mischief.

In what shop, or operatory the fairies make their enchantment, the old wives have not determined. But the operatories of the clergy are well enough known to be the universities, that received their discipline from authority pontifical.

When the fairies are displeased with any body, they are said to send their elves, to pinch them. The ecclesiastics, when they are displeased with any civil state, make also their elves, that is, superstitious, enchanted subjects, to pinch their princes, by preaching sedition; or one prince enchanted with promises, to pinch another.

The fairies marry not; but there be amongst them incubi, that have copulation with flesh and blood. The priests also marry not.

The ecclesiastics take the cream of the land, by donations of ignorant men, that stand in awe of them, and by tithes. So also it is in the fable of fairies, that they enter into the dairies, and feast upon the cream, which they skim from the milk.

What kind of money is current in the kingdom of fairies, is not recorded in the story. But the ecclesiastics in their receipts accept of the same money that we do; though when they are to make any payment, it is in canonizations, indulgencies, and masses.

To this, and such like resemblances between the papacy, and the kingdom of fairies, may be added this, that as the fairies have no existence, but in the fancies of ignorant people, rising from the traditions of old wives, or old poets: so the spiritual power of the Pope, without the bounds of his own civil dominion, consisteth only in the fear that seduced people stand in, of their excommunications; upon hearing of false miracles, false traditions, and false interpretations of the Scripture.

It was not therefore a very difficult matter, for Henry VIII by his exorcism; nor for queen Elizabeth by hers, to cast them out. But who knows that this spirit of Rome, now gone out, and walking by missions through the dry places of China, Japan, and the Indies, that yield him little fruit, may not return, or rather an assembly of spirits worse than he, enter, and inhabit this clean swept house, and make the end thereof worse than the beginning? For it is not the Roman clergy only, that pretends the kingdom of God to be of this world, and thereby to have a power therein, distinct from that of the civil state. And this is all I had a design to say, concerning the doctrine of the politics. Which when I have reviewed, I shall willingly expose it to the censure of my country.

ABOUT THE AUTHOR

Alan Ryan was born in London in 1940 and educated at Oxford University, where he taught for many years. He was professor of politics at Princeton University from 1988 to 1996, and warden of New College, Oxford University, and professor of political theory from 1996 until 2009. He is the author of *The Philosophy of John Stuart Mill*, *The Philosophy of the Social Sciences*, *J. S. Mill*, *Property and Political Theory*, *Bertrand Russell: A Political Life*, *John Dewey and the High Tide of American Liberalism*, *Liberal Anxieties and Liberal Education*, and *On Politics*. He is married to Kate Ryan.